NARROWBOATING FOR NOVICES

Everything you need to know for a successful
holiday on the UK canal network

by

John & Annie Henshaw

Sphinx House Publishing

Published by Sphinx House Publishing
East Sussex BN2 8FL

Book Typesetting & Cover Setup by Velin@Perseus-Design.com

ISBN: 978-0-9930739-9-1

For Pauline & Ray
with thanks for all their
encouragement

NOTE

We have done our best to ensure that everything in this book is accurate.

However, if you find something that you believe to be an error, please let us know on narrowboating@sphinxhouse.com

and we'll endeavour to correct it in the next edition.

CONTENTS

PART THREE: ONTO THE CANAL

INTRODUCTION

Narrowboating is a holiday like no other. It can be incredibly relaxing, very energetic, extremely interesting and great fun . . . and all within half an hour of leaving the marina! You get a view of the countryside and of wildlife that you can get no other way and find interesting places that you never even knew existed.

And a narrowboat is a boat like no other. Motor boats are about speed - but the maximum speed on a canal is 4mph. And sailing is about getting out on the sea 'away from it all' - but on a canal you're never more than a few feet from land. In addition, it's not about getting anywhere but, rather, about the journey itself. We've found that travelling for no more than about five or six hours a day is the ideal. That gives you plenty of time to stop in an isolated spot and enjoy the countryside while you have a cup of coffee or eat your lunch, and to explore any interesting places you come to along the way (and there are plenty of those). If you're the sort of person who likes to push on, trying to get from A to B, then you'd probably be better off with a motoring holiday. Narrowboating is about taking your time, going slowly and relaxing.

That said, it's worth having an idea in advance of how far you might be able to go so that you can plan any particular stops you want to make.

We've written this book in the hope that it will ensure that you get the most out of your first narrowboating holiday and that, like us, you'll go back, time after time after time.

PART ONE

DECIDING WHERE TO GO

There are several things to take into consideration when deciding where to go. First, of course, is the part of the country you fancy. There are navigable canals in England, Wales and Scotland, so there's a lot of choice. Some take you through open countryside, some offer spectacular views. Others alternate open country with pretty villages or built up areas whose waterside buildings are a reminder of the heyday of the canals, when they were used extensively to transport coal, pottery and other goods around the country.

The second consideration is how energetic you are feeling. Some canals are fairly flat and have few locks. Others have a lot of locks, including flights (a series of locks one after the other). These can be very hard work. If you tire easily or you want a really restful holiday, choose a canal, or stretch of canal, with just a few locks - enough to make it interesting but not so many that you're aching from head to foot by the end of the day.

And, finally, you need to decide whether you want to do a 'there and back' or a 'ring'. There are some short rings (mostly within the Birmingham Canal Navigations) but most rings take ten to fourteen days, or more, to complete. We would suggest that you start with a 'there and back' trip. Narrowboat hire companies work on fairly tight schedules - you will need to return your boat quite early on your last day. If you're doing a ring and you find you're a bit behind schedule, you'll be under pressure to get back on time, making the last two or three days less pleasurable than they should be. However, if you plan to go from A to C and back again and, by the half way point, you find yourself only at B, then you can just turn round there. And while three days up and three days back on the same canal may sound a bit dull, it isn't. The canal looks different from the opposite direction and you'll find new places to moor - but you can also revisit places (particularly pubs or restaurants) that you enjoyed on the way out.

In the following section you will find descriptions of a large number of canals, and one or two 'navigations' (waterways that combine sections of canal with sections of river). However, until you're an experienced narrowboater, we suggest that you avoid going on tidal rivers, and even the non-tidal sections of large rivers such as the Severn and the Trent below

Nottingham, where it's far more difficult to control the boat than it is on a canal or narrower non-tidal section of a river.

Once you've decided on a canal, have a look to see which companies hire out boats on that canal and which marina they're based at. And, having booked your trip, you can start planning your holiday. Do remember, however, that narrowboating is becoming more and more popular, particularly since there have been so many programmes about it on television. If you want to go on a particular week and have no other options, you need to book really early (several months in advance) to make sure you get it.

Maps and guides

While your hire company will give you a map to take on the boat, it's always a good idea to have your own, because then you can get an idea of your route before you go. You can also find an excellent map on the the Canal & River Trust (CRT) website:

https://canalrivertrust.org.uk/enjoy-the-waterways/canal-and-river-network

You can either click on the map to see the part of the country you're interested in, or you can click 'View list' and then click on the name of the canal you want to travel on. However, do be aware that a few English canals (such as the Bridgewater) and all the Scottish canals are regulated by authorities other than the CRT and so, while their course will be marked on the CRT map, there will be no details.

For their own canals, the CRT map shows you where there are locks, bridges, aqueducts, moorings, marinas winding holes (places to turn round), water points and much more. You may need to zoom in to maximum to see some of these. This map is not printable but, if you go to:

http://data-canalrivertrust.opendata.arcgis.com/

and scroll down, you will find a list of 'Open apps', one of which is called 'Reference Map'. Click this and it will bring you to a map which is printable. However, once again, you need to zoom in considerably to get all the detail.

The CRT main map will also show any problems affecting your canal (such as repair works) so it's a good idea to have a look at it just before you leave home. You may be able to access it once you're underway, but on most parts of the canal network it's difficult or impossible to get an internet connection.

A large scale paper map can also help you plan your trip - and you'll still have it to refer to when you're on the canal! Two of the most popular are:

- Jane Cumberlidge: *Map of the Inland Waterways of Great Britain* published by Imray, Laurie, Norie & Wilson. ISBN 978-1846238277
- *Collins Nicholson Inland Waterways Map of Great Britain* ISBN 978-0008146535

New editions of each are published at regular intervals.

We have used both these maps. The first distinguishes clearly the broad canals from the narrow ones and shows distances, the number of locks and any restricting dimensions. The second, which is based on Ordnance Survey maps, gives more detail (for example, it indicates the tunnels and locks that need to be booked in advance) and has insets of the Birmingham Canal Navigations, the Scottish inland waterways, and the London area. However, the print is somewhat smaller than that of the Cumberlidge, making it a little harder to read.

For maps of individual canals, those produced by Heron are excellent. They offer a wealth of information on - among other things - visitor moorings, marinas, shops, post offices, pubs, nature reserves, navigation and local history. However, they seem only to be updated occasionally.

As to guides . . . if, like us, you become keen narrowboaters, you will probably finish up with shelves of the things! There are lots to choose from. But there are two main publishers: Nicholson and J.M.Pearson & Son. They both produce guides that give detailed information on locks, tunnels, moorings and winding holes, as well as facilities on and near to the canal such as pubs, restaurants, shops and places to visit. With so many rural shops and pubs closing these days, the guides can get out of date quite quickly, so always make sure you have the latest version.

The maps in the Nicholson's books are based on Ordnance Survey maps (2 inches to 1 mile or roughly 3cm to 1 km). So they give very good and accurate details of the country up to a mile either side of the canal. In addition, they are always arranged with north at the top of each map. Pearson's guides are much more stylised, with each section of the canal drawn horizontally across the page. This can be confusing at times. If the canal twists and turns a lot (and many of them do), the direction of north can change with every page. However, they are probably better than Nicholson's at showing important features on and near the canal.

PART TWO

CHOOSING A CANAL

In this section we have covered the information you need to help you choose your canal - including the number of locks, the type of countryside it passes through, and nearby attractions that you may want to visit. We have not listed all the canals in the UK - we have left out those that are only partly navigable, some that don't link up with other waterways, and some that are very short. Also, we haven't given you all the information there is about a every canal we've listed (if you want more, try one of the guides mentioned in the previous section) but we have tried to include everything you need to know to help you make a choice.

Some attractions we've listed are within walking distance of the canal, others would entail cycling (see Part Three) or a bus trip. Some places, such as Birmingham and Wolverhampton, have two or more canals running through them or meeting there. In such cases, we have listed attractions under the canal that they are closest to or, if very close to two canals, under both. We have tried not to overload the sketch maps with information so, while attractions that are isolated are marked, those in large cities such as Derby or Worcester tend not to be shown individually. However, we have given postcodes wherever possible and suggest you use Google maps to find the best way of getting to the place you want to visit. We have also given website addresses where available. Please check these for opening times and entrance charges.

THE AIRE & CALDER NAVIGATION

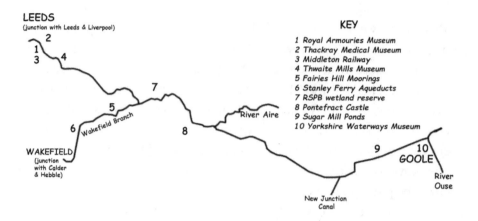

The Aire & Calder Navigation was opened in 1704, is 34 miles long and has 11 locks. It has one branch, the Wakefield, which is 7½ miles long and has 4 locks. The main line begins in Leeds (where it links with the Leeds & Liverpool Canal) and ends at Goole Docks (where it meets the River Ouse). The Wakefield branch leaves the main line at Castleford Junction and ends, naturally enough, in Wakefield, where it meets the Calder & Hebble Canal.

The Aire & Calder also links to the River Aire, at Bank Dole Junction, and to the New Junction Canal, at East Cowick. The section between Wakefield and Leeds is part of two cruising rings - the Outer Pennine Ring (with the Leeds & Liverpool Canal and the Huddersfield Canals) and the North Pennine Ring (with the Leeds & Liverpool and Rochdale Canals).

The eastern section of the Aire & Calder has long straight stretches, mainly through flat agricultural land, while the western section tends to twist gently and has more the look of a river.

At the millenium, it was still carrying over 1½ million tonnes of freight a year and, while this has reduced considerably since then, it still has a fair amount of commercial traffic (which always has right of way).

Most of the locks on the main line are manned by lock-keepers some of the time, but many also have a 'self-serve' operation. Most of these require a CRT key (check with your hire company that you have been provided with this). Detailed instructions on how to use the key can be found on the console that controls the lock. All the locks on the main line have lights which indicate the status of the lock.

In passing: things to see and do

Places of note on the Wakefield branch:

- **Fairies Hill Moorings** near Castleford are on the site of a former coal wharf where the rectangular iron tub-boats known as 'tom puddings' were filled with coal to be transported, usually in trains of 15 or more, to Goole.
- **The Stanley Ferry aqueducts.** One of these, built between 1836 and 1839, is the largest cast iron aqueduct in the world, with a seven-segment arch on each side from which is hung the iron trough. It is 165 feet long and is floodlit at night. The other aqueduct, which is wider, was built in 1981. Next to the aqueduct are the workshops where the gates for broad canals are made.

Places to visit from the main line:
(For more places in Leeds, see the listings in the section on the Leeds & Liverpool Canal.)

- **The Henry Moore Institute, Leeds,** houses one of the largest sculpture exhibitions in Europe.
  74 The Headrow, Leeds LS1 3AH
  https://www.henry-moore.org/visit/henry-moore-institute
- **Leeds Art Gallery** houses a collection of 20th century British art that is recognised as being "of national importance".
  The Headrow, Leeds LS1 3AA
- **Leeds City Museum** has six galleries including natural history and archaeology, as well as special exhibitions and activities.
  Millennium Square, Leeds LS2 8BH
  http://www.leedsmuseum.co.uk/
- **The Royal Armouries Museum** has what is claimed to be the world's best collection of arms & armour, moved here in 1996 from the Tower of London. (You can moor very close, in the basin by Leeds Lock.)
  Armouries Drive, Leeds LS10 1LT
- **The Thackray Medical Museum.** Once a workhouse, this 150 year old grade II listed building is the only museum of its kind in the north of

England. Nine interactive galleries follow the development of medicine and surgery from the Victorian age to the present day.

Beckett Street, Leeds LS9 7LN

http://www.thackraymedicalmuseum.co.uk/

- **Middleton Railway** is the oldest working railway in the world, having been established in 1758. Here you can see industrial steam and diesel railway locomotives and other objects illustrating the history of this railway and of others like it. Trains only run at the weekends.

  Moor Road Railway Station, Moor Road, Leeds LS10 2JQ

  http://www.middletonrailway.org.uk/

- **Thwaite Mills Industrial Museum.** Built in 1823 this is a fully restored working water-powered mill.

  Thwaite Lane, Leeds LS10 1RP

- **RSPB wetland reserve near Castleford** at Newton Ings and Fairburn Ings (Ings is the Old Norse word for 'water meadows' or 'marshes'). Three main trails run through a variety of habitats allowing views of birds such as willow tits, tree sparrows, lapwings, snipe and redshanks and, in the winter, swans, ducks and geese.

  Visitor Centre, Newton Lane, Castleford WF10 2BH

- **Pontefract Castle.** Now a ruin, during the Middle Ages this was one of the most important fortresses in the north of England, becoming a royal castle in 1399. Richard II was imprisoned here and it was besieged three times during the Civil War. There is an exhibition telling the story of the castle and its owners.

  Castle Chain, Pontefract WF8 1QH

- **Sugar Mill Ponds Nature Reserve, Goole.** By Bridge 23 (Rawcliffe Bridge). Water voles have been seen here, as well as some 70 species of birds including great crested grebe, kingfisher, great spotted woodpecker and barn owl.

  Bridge Lane, Goole DN14 8RY

- **The Yorkshire Waterways Museum, Goole,** tells the history of the Aire & Calder Navigation, its role in creating the port and town of Goole, and the 'tom puddings' that transported coal from Yorkshire through Goole Docks to London and the continent.

  Dutch River Side, DN14 5TB

  http://www.waterwaysmuseum.org.uk/

THE ASHBY-DE-LA-ZOUCH CANAL

SNARESTONE
Snarestone Tunnel
• Battlefield Line Railway
Carlton Bridge
MARKET BOSWORTH
SHENTON • Bosworth Field Visitor Centre
DADLINGTON
STOKE GOLDING
HINCKLEY
Coventry Canal
BURTON HASTINGS
MARSTON JUNCTION

Originally 31 miles long, this canal was opened in 1804 to connect the coal mining district around Moira, just outside Ashby-de-la-Zouch, with the Coventry Canal at Marston Junction. Nowadays only 22 miles of the canal are navigable, between Marston Junction and Snarestone. It is a pretty, mostly rural canal, with no locks. However, it has shallow sides which makes mooring difficult. In some of the fields at the side of the canal it is still possible to see the ridge and furrow patterns created by mediaeval farmers.

Hinckley, the only built-up part of the canal, has some fine timber framed cottages and was the home of Joseph Hansom who designed the Hansom cab.

Most of the bridges over the canal are made of stone, with high wide arches, and four of them are grade II listed structures. There is a short, crooked tunnel, 250 yards long, at Snarestone.

This is a wonderful canal on which to observe wildlife - you may see kingfishers, herons, wrens and water voles as well as the more familiar moorhens. The five mile section between Snarestone and Bridge 44 (Carlton Bridge) is a Site of Special Scientific Interest and a habitat for several varieties of dragonfly. The canal is also well stocked with fish, including bream, roach, chub and pike (but do remember that, if you want to fish, you will probably need to apply for a licence).

In passing: things to see and do

- **The Battlefield Line Railway** is all that is left of the Ashby & Nuneaton Joint Railway. It runs steam trains on a five mile trip from Shackerstone to Shenton, via Market Bosworth. The station is near Bridge 52.
Shackerstone Station, Shackerstone CV13 6NW
https://www.battlefieldline.co.uk/

- **St. Botolph's Church, Burton Hastings.** Much of the building dates from the 14th century. The nave was rebuilt in the 16th. There have been some renovations recently. Two ancient iron bound chests in the nave, each made out of a hollowed tree trunk, were probably used to hold parish records.
Mill Lane, Burton Hastings CV11 6XT
http://stbotolphsbh.org.uk/

- **St. Margaret's Church, Stoke Golding,** was built between 1290 and 1340 and is said to be one of the most beautiful churches in Leicestershire. It has an early 14th century octagonal font, box pews, and a Victorian screen. The first Tudor monarch, Henry VII, was crowned nearby in 1485, after the defeat of Richard III at Bosworth.
Stoke Golding CV13 6HD

- **St. James' Church, Dadlington,** dates from the early 12th century. In 1511 Henry VIII authorised the founding of a chantry chapel here to commemorate those killed at the Battle of Bosworth Field in 1485.
The Green, Dadlington CV13 6JB

- **The Bosworth Field Visitor Centre** stands at the site of the Battle of Bosworth Field where Richard III was killed. An interactive exhibition tells the story of the battle and the discovery of the true location of the battlefield.
Ambion Lane, Sutton Cheney CV13 0AD
http://www.bosworthbattlefield.org.uk/

- **Market Bosworth** is a market town with some fine thatched cottages.

THE BIRMINGHAM CANAL NAVIGATIONS (BCN)

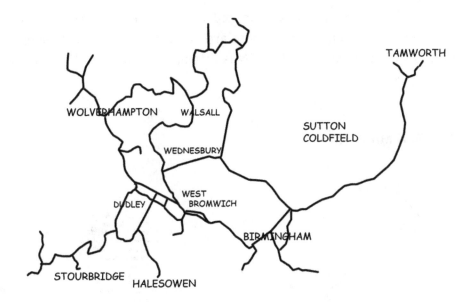

The Birmingham Canal Navigations, or BCN, is an extensive network of canals that connect the cities of Birmingham and Wolverhampton and extends through much of the West Midlands. Just over 100 miles of these canals are navigable. And, yes, it's true - Birmingham does have more canals than Venice.

The first canal to be built in the area was the Birmingham Canal, which was completed in 1772. For nearly 200 years there was a thriving freight trade but ultimately this dwindled and in the mid 20th century 54 miles of canals were closed.

To the north, the BCN links with the Staffordshire & Worcestershire Canal, to the south with the Worcester & Birmingham, to the east with the Coventry Canal, to the south east with the Grand Union Canal and to the south west with the Stourbridge.

Various stretches of the BCN form part of the Black Country Ring (together with the Staffordshire & Worcestershire and the Trent & Mersey Canals) and part of the Avon Ring (with the Worcester & Birmingham and Stratford Canals and the Severn and Avon rivers). Much of the BCN Main Line forms part of the Stourport Ring (with the River Severn, the Staffordshire & Worcestershire, Stourbridge and Worcester & Birmingham Canals, and two other sections of the BCN - the Dudley Canals and the Netherton Tunnel Branch Canal).

In its heyday the BCN consisted of 20 canals and 11 branches and loops. However, many of these are no longer navigable. Although much of what remains of the BCN is urban, there is also a lot of open countryside.

THE BCN MAIN LINE

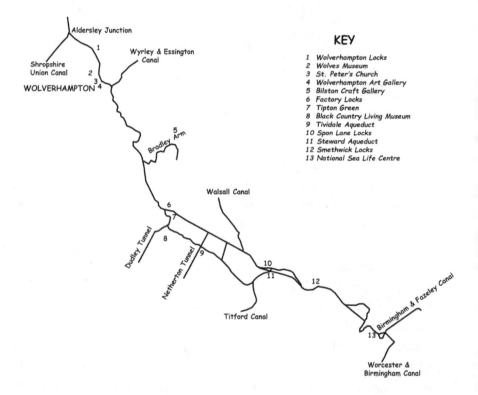

KEY

1 Wolverhampton Locks
2 Wolves Museum
3 St. Peter's Church
4 Wolverhampton Art Gallery
5 Bilston Craft Gallery
6 Factory Locks
7 Tipton Green
8 Black Country Living Museum
9 Tividale Aqueduct
10 Spon Lane Locks
11 Steward Aqueduct
12 Smethwick Locks
13 National Sea Life Centre

Originally called the Birmingham Canal, the Main Line runs from Aldersley Junction, north of Wolverhampton, to Gas Street Basin in central Birmingham. Designed by James Brindley it was ultimately found to be too meandering and was redesigned by Thomas Telford who straightened its route using cuttings and tunnels and, in so doing , took seven miles off its original length. The northern stretch, from Wolverhampton to the Factory Locks at Tipton, plus the looping section that was bypassed, is now known as the Old Main Line, while the straightened section of canal running from the Factory Locks to Birmingham is the New Main Line.

The entire Main Line, from Wolverhampton to Birmingham, is 15½ miles long and the Old Main Line loop is 6½ miles long. There is a flight of 21 locks at the Wolverhampton end of the canal, before it links with the Staffordshire & Worcestershire Canal, and there are three locks at Tipton - the Factory Locks - on the New Main Line. As you proceed towards Birmingham, the construction of the New Main Line means that there is a choice of locks. You can either use the Spon Lane Locks or continue a little further on to where the two Main Lines finally join at the Smethwick Locks. Whichever way you go it's three locks but most people prefer to use the Smethwick Locks, since use of the Spon Lane Locks requires you to negotiate a very tight turn. At its Birmingham end the Main Line links with the Birmingham & Fazeley Canal, which is also part of the BCN.

The Main Line has been described as "Not the prettiest of canals but interesting in many ways". Certainly, if you're interested in industrial history and architecture, there is a lot to see.

In passing: things to see and do

Places of note:

- **Tipton Green**, located between the Old and New Main Lines was the home of the 19th century prize fighter William Perry, whose parents were bargees. He was known as the Tipton Slasher and there is a statue of him on the green.
- **The Tividale Aqueduct.** Much of this aqueduct, which takes the Old Main Line over the Netherton Tunnel Branch, has been constructed using blue engineering bricks known locally as 'toccy bricks'. These bricks were made from Staffordshire clay which was baked in the hottest part of the oven to make them practically impervious to water.
- **Spon Lane Top Lock** has a roving bridge over it (see Glossary).
- **The Steward Aqueduct** carries the Old Main Line over the New, close to the Spon Lane top lock. Consisting of an iron trough, it was completed in 1828 and is grade II listed.
- **Smethwick Top Lock** has a small hexagonal toll booth next to it - a replica of the original that once stood here.
- **The Engine Arm Aqueduct** near the Spon Lane Junction was completed in 1825 and is a scheduled ancient monument.

- **The Tap and Spile pub** at the Gas Street Basin in Birmingham dates from 1821.

Places to visit:

- **Wolves Museum** is an interactive museum that tells the story of Wolverhampton Wanderers and modern football.
  Molineux Stadium, Waterloo Rd, Wolverhampton WV1 4QR
  http://www.wolvesmuseum.co.uk/
- **St. Peter's Collegiate Church, Wolverhampton,** was founded in 994, but the oldest part of the building probably dates from 1200. The church was extended in the 14th and 15th centuries. The west gallery was added in 1610 and there was extensive restoration in the 19th century. The font and several stone figures date from the late 15th century and there is an unusual stone pulpit with a carved lion. A 14 foot high stone column carved with birds and animals, dating from the 9th century, stands near the south porch.
  Lich Gates, Wolverhampton, WV1 1TY
- **Wolverhampton Art Gallery** has paintings spanning 300 years and one of the best collections of Pop Art outside London.
  Lichfield Street, Wolverhampton, WV1 1DU
- **The Bilston Craft Gallery** has collections of locally made decorative objects from the 18th century to the present day, including one of the finest collections in the country of English painted enamels.
  Mount Pleasant, Wolverhampton, WV14 7LU
- **The Black Country Living Museum** has a recreation of a 19th century industrial town and is one of the largest open air museums in the UK.
  2 Tipton Road, Dudley DY1 4SQ
  http://www.bclm.co.uk/
- **The National Sea Life Centre** has over 60 displays of freshwater and marine life and the only fully transparent 360 degree underwater tunnel in the UK. Its one million litre ocean tank is home to giant green sea turtles, blacktip reef sharks and tropical reef fish.
  The Waters Edge, Brindley Place, Birmingham B1 2HL
  https://www.visitsealife.com/birmingham/

THE BIRMINGHAM & FAZELEY CANAL

KEY

1 Digbeth Canal
2 Farmers Bridge Locks
3 Aston Locks
4 Ashted Tunnel & Locks
5 Birmingham Museum & Art Gallery
   St. Philip's Cathedral
   St. Chad's RC Cathedral
   Thinktank
6 The Pen Museum
7 Museum of the Jewellery Quarter
8 Aston Hall
9 Drayton Manor Swing & Foot Bridges

This canal starts at the Old Turn Junction in Birmingham (near the National Indoor Arena) and runs for 15 miles to Fazeley Junction, just outside Tamworth. The main canal has 38 locks including the Farmer's Bridge Flight of 13 locks, and the Aston and Curdworth Flights, each of which has 11 locks. Just before the Aston Locks, the one mile long Digbeth Branch Canal runs to join the Grand Union Canal at Warwick Bar. The Digbeth has six locks and a grade II listed tunnel which is 103 yards long. There is another short tunnel on the main line at Curdworth (57 yards long). Unusually, the bridges on this canal are not numbered, although they all have names. Handcuff keys are required for many of the locks - you need to ensure that your hire company has supplied you with these.

The canal links with the Tame Valley Canal and the Grand Union Canal at Salford Junction, the Coventry Canal at Fazeley Junction, and the Worcester & Birmingham Canal and the BCN Main Line at the Old Turn Junction. Together with the Coventry, Oxford, Grand Union and Stratford-upon-Avon Canals, it forms the Warwickshire Ring. It also forms part of the Black Country Ring, with the Staffordshire & Worcestershire Canal, the Trent & Mersey Canal and other sections of the BCN.

Although some of the canal goes through urban areas, there is still quite a lot of countryside to be seen.

In passing: things to see and do

Places of note:

- **Farmer's Bridge Locks and Aston Locks** take the canal down 150 feet in less than three miles. Once some of the busiest locks on the canal system, they used to be gas lit so they could be used at night.
- **Salford Junction.** Here the canal runs directly under the Gravelly Hill Interchange - better known as Spaghetti Junction.
- **Drayton Manor Swing Bridge** has an unusual Gothic style footbridge next to it, with castellated towers and a spiral staircase at each end.

Places to visit:

- **Birmingham Museum and Art Gallery** holds an outstanding collection of pre-Raphaelite and other paintings, as well as silverware, sculpture, metalwares, glass, ceramics and a collection of Egyptian mummies and coffins. One gallery is devoted to the Staffordshire Hoard, the largest hoard of Anglo-Saxon gold ever found.
  Chamberlain Square B3 3DH
  http://www.birminghammuseums.org.uk/bmag
- **St. Philip's Anglican Cathedral.** Built in 1715, it became a cathedral in 1905. It has a superb set of stained glass windows by Edward Burne-Jones.
  Colmore Row, Birmingham B3 2QB
  http://www.birminghamcathedral.com/
- **St. Chad's Roman Catholic Cathedral** is one of the finest neo-gothic churches in England. It was designed by Augustus Pugin and opened in 1841. It contains a late mediaeval statue of the Virgin Mary, a 16th century Flemish pulpit and some fine 19th century stained glass.
  Queensway, Birmingham B4 6EU
  http://www.stchadscathedral.org.uk/
- **Thinktank Birmingham Science Museum** has over 200 hands-on exhibits and a state-of-the-art planetarium.
  Millennium Point, Curzon Street B4 7XG
  http://www.birminghammuseums.org.uk/thinktank

- **The Pen Museum** is housed in a grade II listed former pen factory, a reminder of the time when Birmingham was the centre of the pen-manufacturing world.
Unit 3, The Argent Centre, 60, Frederick Street, Hockley B1 3HS
http://penmuseum.org.uk/
- **The Museum of the Jewellery Quarter** tells the story of Birmingham's jewellery and metalworking heritage, with live demonstrations of traditional skills.
75-79 Vyse Street, Hockley B18 6HA
http://www.birminghammuseums.org.uk/jewellery
- **Aston Hall. Built** between 1618 and 1635, this grade I listed building is one of England's finest Jacobean mansions. It has some fine interiors, with early 17th century plasterwork, wood carving and chimney pieces, and room displays from the 17th, 18th and 19th centuries.
Trinity Road, Aston B6 6JD
http ://www.birminghammuseums.org.uk/aston
- **Drayton Manor Theme Park and Zoo** offers white-knuckle rides, a 15 acre zoo, and 'Thomas Land' with all the characters from Thomas the Tank Engine.
Drayton Manor Drive, Fazeley, Mile Oak B78 3TW
https://www.draytonmanor.co.uk/

THE NETHERTON TUNNEL BRANCH CANAL & DUDLEY CANALS

The Netherton Tunnel Canal is only 2½ miles long, has no locks, and links the BCN Main Line with the Dudley No. 2 Canal. Its interest is in its tunnel which, at 3027 yards long, forms most of the branch. It was the last canal to be built in Britain during the canal heyday and was opened in 1858. It is 27 feet wide, allowing two-way traffic, and it has the largest cross section of any canal tunnel in the country. Brick lined throughout, it has a towpath on each side which originally meant that the boats could be towed through by their horses, rather than having to be 'legged' through. The eastern wall has distance markers and the tunnel used to be fitted with gas lighting. It is ventilated by openings covered by iron grilles over which are brick structures known locally as 'pepper pots'.

The Dudley Canal Line No 1 is 4½ miles long, has 12 locks and a 1¾ mile long tunnel, and runs from Tipton Junction to Delph Bottom Lock, thus connecting the BCN Old Main Line with the Stourbridge Canal. The Dudley Canal Line No 2 meets the Dudley Canal Line No 1 at Parkhead Junction and finishes, after a run of 5½ miles, at Hawne Basin. It has no locks.

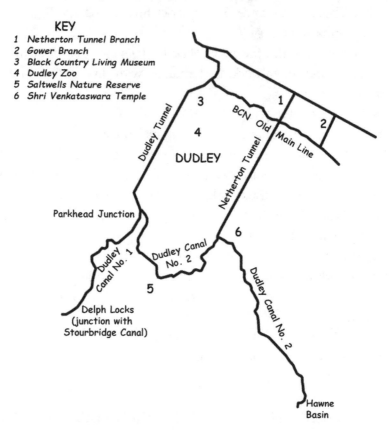

KEY
1 Netherton Tunnel Branch
2 Gower Branch
3 Black Country Living Museum
4 Dudley Zoo
5 Saltwells Nature Reserve
6 Shri Venkataswara Temple

In passing: places to visit

- **The Black Country Living Museum** (see BCN Main Line)
  2 Tipton Road, Dudley DY1 4SQ
  http://www.bclm.co.uk/
- **Dudley Zoo and Castle.** The 40 acre site includes a ruined 11th century castle and limestone caverns as well as an important animal collection linked to international conservation and breeding programmes. Endangered species include Asiatic lions, Sumatran tigers, Bornean orang-utans, Tibetan red pandas, and Humboldt penguins.
  Castle Hill, Dudley DY1 4QF
  http://www.dudleyzoo.org.uk/

- **Saltwells Local Nature Reserve.** Covering 247 acres, this is one of the UK's largest urban nature reserves. At different times of the year you can see treecreepers, jays, great spotted woodpeckers, water rails, snipe, teal, linnets and reed buntings, while common spotted and southern marsh orchids are to be found in the old claypit which was closed in the 1940s. Saltwells Lane, off Coppice Lane, Quarry Bank, Dudley DY5 1AX
- **Shri Venkateswara Temple.** A large and beautiful Hindu temple complex, opened in 2006. Guided tours have to be booked. Shoes have to be removed before entering the temple. 101 Dudley Road East, Tividale, Dudley B69 3DU http://www.venkateswara.org.uk/

THE WALSALL CANAL

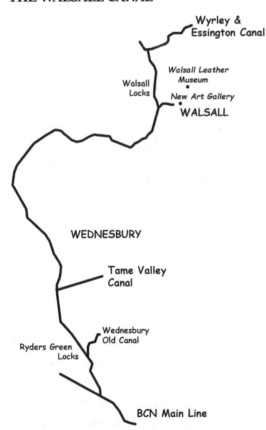

This canal runs through the Black Country and, passing round the western side of the city of Walsall, connects the BCN Main Line to the Wyrley & Essington Canal. It is seven miles long.

At the northern end is a flight of eight locks (the Walsall Locks) and at the southern end is another flight of eight (the Ryders Green Locks). The canal meets the Wednesbury Old Canal (only part of which is navigable) at Ryders Green Junction and the Tame Valley Canal at Doe Bank Junction. The very short Walsall own Arm, which branches off just before the Walsall Locks, leads into the city itself. After the locks, the canal meets the Wyrley & Essington Canal at Birchills Junction.

In passing: places to visit

- **The New Art Gallery, Walsall.** An extensive collection of paintings, drawings, sculpture and prints by artists including Picasso, Braque, Gericault and Delacroix.
  Gallery Square, Walsall, WS2 8LG
  http://thenewartgallerywalsall.org.uk/
- **Walsall Leather Museum** tells the story of the Walsall leather trade. With live demonstrations of traditional leather crafts in period workshops.
  Littleton Street West, Walsall WS2 8EQ
  http://cms.walsall.gov.uk/leathermuseum/

THE WYRLEY & ESSINGTON AND CANNOCK EXTENSION CANALS

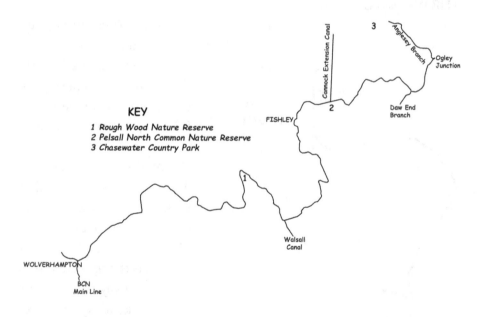

Known locally as "the Curly Wyrley", the Wyrley & Essington was opened in 1797 and originally ran from Wolverhampton to Huddlesford Junction near Lichfield. Nowadays it is only navigable for 16½ miles from Wolverhampton to Ogley Junction near Brownhills. It derives its nickname from the fact that it is a 'contour canal', twisting and turning to avoid any gradients and the need for locks.

Two thirds of the canal, from Wolverhampton to just before Freeth Bridge (at Fishley) is fairly urban, while the rest runs through open countryside.

Few boats use this canal and there is quite a lot of interesting aquatic plant life, including floating water plantain which is protected, since it is rare in the UK.

The canal has connections to the Walsall Canal, at Birchills Junction, and the Cannock Extension Canal at Pelsall Junction. The 1½ mile Anglesey Branch leaves at Ogley Junction and ends close to Chasewater Country Park.

Only the southern section of the Cannock Extension Canal remains. Just under 2 miles long, it leaves the Wyrley & Essington Canal at Pelsall Junction and runs north in a straight line to Norton Canes. Opened in 1863, it is rural and little used. Like the Wyrley & Essington Canal, it has a large population of rare floating water plantain, and it has been designated as a Site of Special Scientific Interest.

In passing: things to see and do

- **Rough Wood Nature Reserve.** Ancient oak woodland and a series of pools. Bloxwich WV12 5NZ
- **Pelsall North Common Nature Reserve** is an area of wet lowland heath with a huge array of wildlife including bats, voles, shrews, foxes, polecats, lizards and great crested newts. There are also numerous heathland plants and flowers including southern marsh and the common spotted orchid.
  Pelsall WS3 5AA (close to the junction with the Cannock Extension Canal)
- **Chasewater Country Park**, at the end of the Anglesey Branch, has a reservoir, a heritage railway, and excellent facilities for bird watching, walking and cycling.
  Pool Lane, Burntwood WS8 7NL

THE TAME VALLEY, DAW END & RUSHALL CANALS

Opened in 1844, the Tame Valley Canal is 8½ miles long and runs from the Tame Valley Junction, where it joins the Walsall Canal, to Salford Junction (underneath Spaghetti Junction) where it meets the Birmingham & Fazeley Canal and the Grand Union Canal. It also links to the Rushall Canal at Rushall Junction.

It boasts eight aqueducts (only one of which is modern) and a flight of 13 locks (the Perry Barr Locks) and it was one of the last narrow canals to be built.

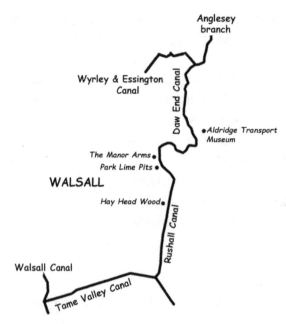

Although the Tame Valley Canal ends in the heart of the Black Country, much of its route is suburban or rural and, with the Rushall Canal, the Daw End Branch Canal and the Wyrley & Essington Canal, if forms a quieter alternative to the BCN Main Line.

The Daw End Branch Canal (pronounced locally as 'Doe End') is one of the most rural canals on the BCN. It is 5½ miles long and has no locks. Leaving the Wyrley & Essington Canal at Catshill Junction, Brownhills, it runs to meet the Rushall Canal at Longwood Junction

The Rushall Canal is a straight, 3 mile long canal which runs along the eastern side of the city of Walsall, connecting the Daw End Branch Canal (which it meets at Longwood Junction) with the Tame Valley Canal (which it meets at Rushall Junction). It has nine locks and, together with the Daw End Branch, is one of the most rural canals in the entire BCN. Although short, it's worth a visit, having pretty gardens, original lock keepers' cottages and traditional canal pubs along the way.

In passing: things to see and do
Places of note:
● **Perry Barr Locks.** The original lock keepers' cottages are still to be seen.

Places to visit:
● **Hay Head Wood Nature Reserve.** The woods surround pools that used to be part of the Daw End canal network. Birds that can be seen here include great spotted woodpeckers, nuthatches, grey herons and kingfishers. The trees include willow and alder.
Longwood Lane, Walsall WS4 2JS

- **Park Lime Pits Nature Reserve.** Two large pools surrounded by mature beech woodland form a home for over 100 species of birds and over 300 species of plants.
Park Road, Walsall WS4 2HH
- **The Manor Arms, Daw End.** Now a pub, this building dates from the early 12th century and has, in its time, been a mill, a monastery and a farmhouse. It is said that Glenn Miller, the band leader, used to drink here during WWII.
Park Road, Walsall WS4 1LG
- **Aldridge Transport Museum** has a wide range of vehicles and transport memorabilia, all with a West Midlands connection.
Shenstone Drive, Northgate, Aldridge WS9 8TP
http://www.amrtm.org/

THE BRIDGEWATER CANAL

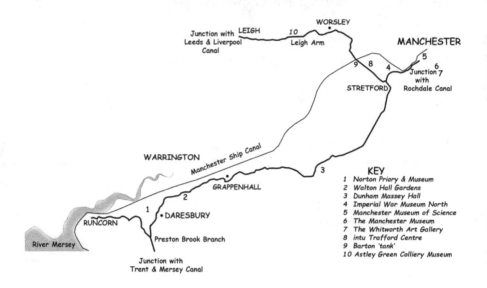

KEY

1 Norton Priory & Museum
2 Walton Hall Gardens
3 Dunham Massey Hall
4 Imperial War Museum North
5 Manchester Museum of Science
6 The Manchester Museum
7 The Whitworth Art Gallery
8 intu Trafford Centre
9 Barton 'tank'
10 Astley Green Colliery Museum

Although not the first canal to be built in Britain (that honour probably belongs to the Foss Dyke in Lincolnshire) the Bridgewater Canal was the first to be built through 'virgin territory' - that is, not following the route of an existing waterway. Completed in 1761, it was named after the man who commissioned it - Francis Egerton, the third Duke of Bridgewater, who used it to transport coal from his mines at Worsley to Manchester.

The canal is 28 miles long and runs from Castlefield Junction in Manchester (where it connects with the Rochdale Canal) to Runcorn in Cheshire. It has no locks, and nor does either of its branches - the Leigh Arm, which is just under 11 miles long and runs from Stretford to Leigh (where it meets the Leigh Arm of the Leeds & Liverpool Canal) and the Preston Brook Branch (which is three quarters of a mile long and connects to the Trent & Mersey Canal).

Together with the Ashton, Peak Forest, Macclesfield and Trent & Mersey Canals, the Bridgewater forms part of the Cheshire Ring. It also links to the Manchester Ship Canal through the Pomona Lock in Manchester.

Much of the Bridgewater Canal is rural or suburban, and grey herons, song thrushes, reed buntings, kingfishers and white throats have all been seen, as well as orange tip and painted lady butterflies.

In passing: things to see and do

Things to see:

- **Castlefield viaducts.** These are Victorian cast iron viaducts that cross the canal basin in the centre of Manchester.
- **The Barton 'Tank'.** An important piece of Victorian civil engineering, and now a grade II listed building, this mechanical swing aqueduct was built in the 1890's to take the Leigh Arm across the Manchester Ship Canal.

Places to visit from the main branch, between Runcorn and Manchester:

- **Norton Priory Museum and Gardens.** Founded as an abbey in 1134 and closed down in 1536 by Henry VIII, this is the most excavated monastic site in Europe. Later it became a manor house. It now houses the largest exhibition of mediaeval monastic life in Britain. The 18th century walled garden is surrounded by woodland and a wild flower meadow.
  Tudor Road, Windmill Hill, Runcorn WA7 1SX
  http://nortonpriory.org/
- **Daresbury.** Lewis Carroll was born here in 1832. To celebrate the centenary of his birth, a stained glass window showing characters from Alice's Adventures in Wonderland was installed in All Saints' Church where his father was once the vicar.
- **Walton Hall Gardens** have trees and shrubs from all over the world, together with a children's zoo, a pitch 'n' putt and a cycle museum.
  Walton Lea Road, Higher Walton WA4 6SN
  https://www.warrington.gov.uk/waltongardens
- **Grappenhall** is a village with cobbled streets, Georgian villas and 18th century cottages
- **St. Wilfrid's Church, Grapenhall,** is grade I listed and dates back to 1120. A carving of a cat on the west face of the tower is believed to have been Lewis Carroll's inspiration for the grinning Cheshire Cat in Alice's Adventures in Wonderland.
  Church Lane, Grapenhall WA4 3EP
- **Dunham Massey Hall** is a National Trust property set in over 300 acres of ancient parkland. It boasts one of Britain's finest winter gardens as well as a superb collection of 18th century furniture and Huguenot silver.
  Woodhouse Lane, Altrincham WA14 4SJ

- **Imperial War Museum North.** Exhibits include a Russian T-34 tank, a United States Marine Corps AV-8B Harrier jet and the 13-pounder field gun that fired the first British shot of WWI.
  The Quays, Trafford Wharf Road, Manchester M17 1TZ
  http://www.iwm.org.uk/visits/iwm-north
- **Manchester Museum of Science & Industry.** The exhibition includes the models used by John Dalton to demonstrate his atomic theory, parts of the world's first commercially available computer, and one of the world's largest collections of working steam mill engines.
  Liverpool Road, Castlefield M3 4FP
  http://msimanchester.org.uk/
- **The Manchester Museum** has exhibitions of archaeology, anthropology and natural history.
  University Of Manchester, Oxford Road M13 9PL
- **The Whitworth Art Gallery.** An internationally important collection of 55,000 artworks.
  Oxford Road, Manchester M15 6ER

Places to visit from the Leigh Arm, between Stretford and Leigh:
- **intu Trafford Centre** is a huge indoor shopping centre and leisure complex with a Legoland Discovery Centre and a large SeaLife Centre.
  intu Trafford Centre, Manchester M17 8AA
  http://intu.co.uk/traffordcentre
- **Worsley** is a village with some beautiful half-timbered houses. The underground canals bringing coal out of the Duke of Bridgewater's mines emerged here, and two of the exits can still be seen at Worsley Delph.
- **Astley Green Colliery Museum.** Exhibits include a collection of 28 colliery locomotives and a steam winding engine.
  Higher Green Lane, Astley Green, Tyldesley M29 7JB

THE CALDER & HEBBLE NAVIGATION

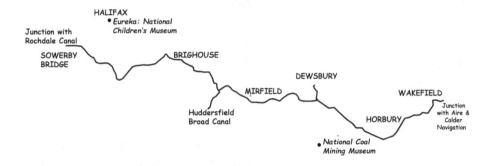

This is a broad waterway - that is to say, it has 14 foot wide locks and bridge openings. It is composed of alternating sections of river and canal.

It is 21 miles long and starts in Wakefield, where it links with the Aire & Calder Navigation, then runs through Mirfield, after which there is a junction with the Huddersfield Broad Canal, and it ends at Sowerby Bridge, where it meets the Rochdale Canal. Much of the route is rural.

The navigation has 39 locks, of which twelve are flood locks. These are designed to prevent the canal from becoming flooded when the river rises above normal levels. They can be left open when levels are normal, allowing the height of the canal to rise and fall with the height of the river.

Although the locks are wide, some of them are very short. Boats longer than 57 feet have to lie diagonally in the locks and, since this is only possible for narrowboats, wide beamed barges longer than this cannot use this navigation. Narrowboats up to 60 feet can manage the locks but, even so, it is not easy (they may need to be poled into position or to go down locks backwards), so an inexperienced crew with a boat longer than 57 feet should avoid using this waterway.

The Calder & Hebble is also unusual in needing a handspike to open the locks. This is a wooden lever which is used rather in the manner of a crowbar to lift the lock paddles. Make sure that your hire company has provided one. A windlass is also needed.

In passing: things to see and do

Places of note:

- **Sowerby Bridge.** There are some fine 200 year old canal buildings at the terminal basin - four stone warehouses, covered docks and the manager's house.
- **Brighouse.** There is a double roving bridge (see Glossary) at the canal basin.

Places to visit:

- **Wakefield Cathedral.** Built in 1329 on the site of a Saxon church and partially rebuilt and enlarged in 1469, the cathedral has fine mediaeval carvings, an unusual font dating from 1661 and the most complete collection of Charles Kempe stained glass in the world.
  Northgate, Wakefield WF1 1HG
  https://www.wakefieldcathedral.org.uk/
- **The Hepworth Art Gallery, Wakefield,** has been described as "One of the finest contemporary art museums in Europe." It holds a collection of sculptures by Barbara Hepworth, and works by other major 20th century British artists.
  Gallery Walk, Wakefield WF1 5AW
  http://www.hepworthwakefield.org/
- **The Smith Art Gallery, Brighouse,** has a permanent exhibition of Victorian paintings and hosts a variety of temporary exhibitions, including many by local and regional artists.
  Halifax Road, Brighouse HD6 2AF
- **The National Mining Museum** (with underground tours). Take a bus from Horbury.
  Caphouse Colliery, New Road, Overton WF4 4RH
  https://www.ncm.org.uk/
- **Eureka: the National Children's Museum** is the only fully interactive museum in the UK that is totally dedicated to children aged 0-11.
  Discovery Road, Halifax HX1 2NE
  https://www.eureka.org.uk/

THE CALDON CANAL

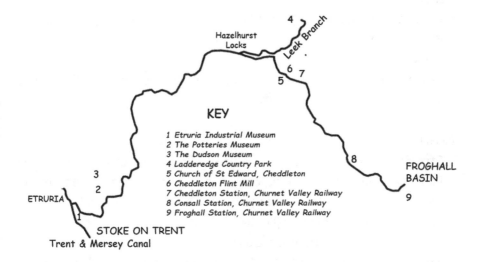

KEY

1 Etruria Industrial Museum
2 The Potteries Museum
3 The Dudson Museum
4 Ladderedge Country Park
5 Church of St Edward, Cheddleton
6 Cheddleton Flint Mill
7 Cheddleton Station, Churnet Valley Railway
8 Consall Station, Churnet Valley Railway
9 Froghall Station, Churnet Valley Railway

Opened in 1779, this canal is 18 miles long, starting at Etruria in Stoke-on-Trent (where it meets the Trent & Mersey Canal) and ending at Froghall Basin in Staffordshire. Although it starts in the heart of the Potteries, it runs through open country, and some spectacular scenery, after Lock 4. It has 17 locks (the first two of which form a staircase) and three lift bridges. Just before it reaches Froghall Basin, the canal goes through a tunnel which, while it is only 76 yards long, has very limited headroom. If you're not sure about tackling this, the last place you can wind (turn) is two miles before the start of the tunnel. See:

http://www.cuct.org.uk/caldon/guide/froghall-tunnel

You will need a handcuff key to open Lock 3 as well as a a CRT key to operate Bridge 11 and Bridge 21 and a windlass to operate Bridge 23. Make sure your hire company supplies you with the necessary keys.

The three mile long Leek Branch is lock-free. Having left the main line just before the Hazelhurst Locks, it then crosses it via the Hazelhurst Aqueduct. It passes through a 130 yard long tunnel and ends close to the Ladderedge Country Park on the outskirts of Leek. Boats more than 45 feet long should not go to the end of the branch but should turn at Bridge 9 where there is more room.

In passing: things to see and do

Places of note:

- **Etruria.** A statue of James Brindley, the engineer who designed many of Britain's canals, stands near the junction of the Caldon and the Trent & Mersey.
- **Froghall Basin.** A peaceful woodland setting with grade II listed lime kilns.

Places to visit from the main line:

- **Etruria Industrial Museum.** The home of Jesse Shirley's 1857 Bone and Flint Mill, the only remaining operational steam driven potters' mill in the world. It has limited opening hours - check before visiting!
  Etruria Vale Road, Etruria ST1 4RB
  http://www.etruriamuseum.org.uk/
- **The Potteries Museum & Art Gallery** houses the Staffordshire Hoard (the largest ever find of Anglo-Saxon treasure) and the world's greatest collection of Staffordshire ceramics, as well as paintings (including works by Picasso, Durer and Degas), natural history and geology exhibits, and a World War II Spitfire.
  Bethesda Street, Stoke-on-Trent ST1 3DW
- **The Dudson Museum** has over 1000 pieces of pottery spanning more than 200 years, including Staffordshire figures, jasperware and relief-moulded stoneware, all housed in a converted grade II listed bottle oven.
  Hope Street, Hanley ST1 5DD
- **The Church of St. Edward the Confessor, Cheddleton,** dates back to the 13th century and has stained glass windows by William Morris and Edward Burne Jones.
  Hollow Lane, Cheddleton ST13 7HP
- **Cheddleton Flint Mill.** A complex of buildings next to the canal includes two water mills, a miller's cottage, two flint kilns, a drying kiln and outbuildings. With foundations probably dating back to the 13th century, corn was milled here until the late 18th century when the South Mill was converted to grind flint (for the pottery industry) and the North Mill was built specifically for that purpose.
  Cheadle Road, Cheddleton ST13 7HL
  http://www.cheddletonflintmill.com/

- **The Churnet Valley Steam Railway** runs from Cheddleton via Consall to Froghall, a round trip of 11 miles through Staffordshire's 'Little Switzerland'. At Cheddleton station, there is an exhibition of artefacts relating to the North Staffordshire Railway.
Cheddleton Station, Basford Bridge Lane, Cheddleton ST13 7EG
Consall Station, Consall ST13 7EE
Kingsley & Froghall Station, Bank View, Froghall ST10 2HA
https://www.churnet-valley-railway.co.uk/

A place to visit from the Leek Branch:
- **Ladderedge Country Park** offers 70 acres of fields and woodland, with ponds, marshland and streams, and some great views over Leek and towards the Peak District.
Sunny Hills Road, Leek ST13 7AA

THE COVENTRY CANAL

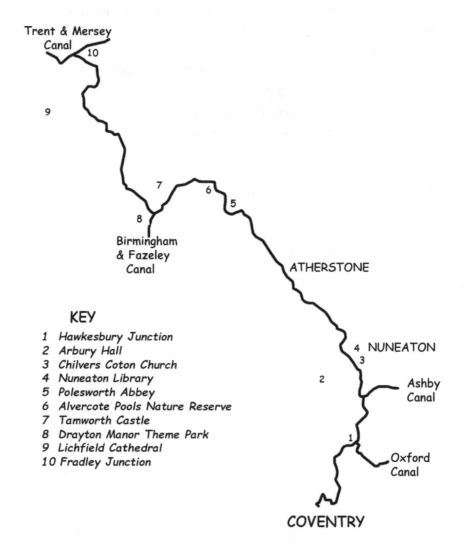

Trent & Mersey
Canal

10

9

7

6

5

8

Birmingham
& Fazeley
Canal

ATHERSTONE

KEY

1 Hawkesbury Junction
2 Arbury Hall
3 Chilvers Coton Church
4 Nuneaton Library
5 Polesworth Abbey
6 Alvercote Pools Nature Reserve
7 Tamworth Castle
8 Drayton Manor Theme Park
9 Lichfield Cathedral
10 Fradley Junction

4 NUNEATON
3

2

Ashby
Canal

1

Oxford
Canal

COVENTRY

This canal starts in Coventry, just north of the city centre, and runs for 38 miles to Fradley Junction, just north of Lichfield, where it joins the Trent & Mersey Canal. Some maps show the canal as having a northern and a southern section, connected by a stretch of the Birmingham & Fazeley Canal, but others describe the whole route as the Coventry Canal.

There are 13 locks and, between Bridges 75 and 76, near Alvercote, there is a short aqueduct over the river Tame. The canal connects to the Oxford Canal at Hawkesbury Junction, the Ashby Canal at Marston Junction and the

Birmingham & Fazeley Canal at Fazeley Junction. Together with the Oxford, Grand Union, Stratford-upon-Avon and Birmingham & Fazeley Canals, the Coventry forms the Warwickshire Ring. With the Grand Union, Oxford, Birmingham & Fazeley and Trent & Mersey Canals, plus the River Trent and the River Soar, it forms the Leicestershire Ring.

Once out of Coventry, much of the canal is rural. After about four miles, the old route of the Oxford Canal can be seen running parallel. At Hawkesbury Junction, there is a sharp turn into the Oxford Canal and longer boats have to approach this very carefully.

In passing: things to see and do

Places of note:

- **Coventry.** At the start of the canal, the Canal Bridge, Canal House and the warehouses are all grade II listed buildings.
- **Cash's 'hundred houses'.** Situated after Bridge 2 (Cash's Lane Bridge), three quarters of a mile after leaving Coventry Basin, are the houses built in 1857 by John & Joseph Cash for their employees. Cash's was the foremost manufacturer of silk ribbons in England (and in the 20th century made woven name-tapes used to mark the clothes of school children all over the UK). The houses had living space on the lower two floors and workrooms on the top floor but only 48 of the proposed 100 were built and only 37 remain.
- **Hawkesbury Junction.** An elegant 50 foot wide bridge spans the junction of the two canals. There are a number of listed buildings here, dating from the heyday of the canals. The pump house dates from 1837. The cottages known as Sutton Stop derived the name from the family that were lock keepers at Hawkesbury from 1807 to 1876.
- **Fradley Junction.** Just before the junction is reached, the canal passes round the upper edge of a World War II airfield, of which only one runway remains. Those who died while stationed here were buried in the local church and their names have been commemorated in road names on the housing estate that now covers a section of the airfield.

Places to visit:

- **Coventry's two cathedrals.** The mediaeval church of St. Michael was designated a cathedral in 1918 but was badly damaged by bombing in 1940.

The new cathedral, designed by Basil Spence was opened in 1962. Works specially commissioned for the cathedral include Graham Sutherland's 'Christ in Glory' (said to be the largest tapestry in the world), John Piper's stained glass Baptistery Window, and Jacob Epstein's bronze statues of St. Michael and the Devil.

Priory Street, Coventry CV1 5FB

- **St. John's Church, Coventry,** was founded in the mid 14th century by the mediaeval Guild of St. John the Baptist. It was closed by Henry VIII in 1546 and, during the Civil War, was used as a prison for Royalist soldiers. The City of Coventry supported the Parliamentarians, and the prisoners were treated harshly - the origin of the saying "sent to Coventry". St. John's was finally restored as a parish church in 1734.

  On the corner of Hill Street & Corporation Street, Coventry CV1 3AY

- **Coventry Transport Museum** is the largest publicly owned collection of British vehicles in the world.

  Millennium Place, Hales Street, Coventry CV1 1JD

  http://www.transport-museum.com/

- **Arbury Hall** is the birthplace of the novelist George Eliot. She used it as the model for Cheverel Manor in Scenes of Clerical Life . Limited opening.

  Griff Lane, Arbury Estate, Nuneaton CV10 7PT

  http://www.arburyestate.co.uk/

- **Chilvers Coton Church.** George Eliot (whose real name was Mary Ann Evans) was baptised here, and the village became 'Shepperton' in her Scenes of Clerical Life , while the nearby town of Nuneaton was 'Milby'. Parts of the church date back to the second half of the 13th century. The church was destroyed by bombs in 1941 and later was rebuilt with the help of German prisoners of war.

  Avenue Road, Chilvers Coton CV11 4NQ

- **Nuneaton Library** has a huge collection of George Eliot memorabilia including photographs, pamphlets and facsimiles of her correspondence as well as over 2000 books. An appointment is needed to view the collection. email: *libraryenquiryteam@warwickshire.gov.uk*

  Church Street, Nuneaton CV11 4DR

- **Atherstone** is a market town with some Georgian buildings. It was a major centre for hat-making between the 17th and 20th centuries. It is famed for its Shrove Tuesday ball game, held annually since the 12th century. A complete free for all, the game is played in the main street. There are no teams and no goals and the only rule is that players are not allowed to kill each other.

- **Polesworth Abbey.** Founded in the 9th century by St. Modwena and King Egbert, the site is now a scheduled ancient monument. All that remains is the 12th century church of St. Editha (the first abbess, and daughter of King Egbert), the 14th century gatehouse and the restored ruins of the cloister.
  High Street, Polesworth B78 1DU

- **Alvercote Pools Nature Reserve.** This Site of Special Scientific Interest was once a stretch of fields along the River Anker. But mining subsidence resulted in the formation of a lake, marshes, swamps and shallow pools that have become the habitat of numerous species of wildlife and flora.
  Between Polesworth and Tamworth, B78 1AS

- **Tamworth Castle.** This Norman motte and bailey castle has a mediaeval gatehouse, Tudor chapel, and more than 15 fully furnished rooms including a 15th century banqueting hall, Jacobean & Tudor apartments, and a haunted bedroom. There is a display of Saxon weapons and other items from the Staffordshire Hoard (the largest hoard of Anglo-Saxon gold ever found).
  Holloway, Ladybank, Tamworth B79 7NA

- **Drayton Manor Theme Park and Zoo** (see Birmingham & Fazeley Canal)
  Drayton Manor Drive, Fazeley, Mile Oak B78 3TW
  https://www.draytonmanor.co.uk/

- **Lichfield Cathedral** is the only English mediaeval cathedral to have three spires (these being known locally as the 'Ladies of the Vale'). Built in the early 14th century, it was damaged during the Civil War and 'restored' in the 19th century by the architect Sir George Gilbert Scott. Among the treasures on display are the 8th century St. Chad Gospels, some items from the Saxon Staffordshire Hoard, the Lichfield angel (a carved limestone panel, discovered under the cathedral nave in 2003 and dating from around 800 AD, which still shows traces of its original pigment) and the Herkenrode stained glass. The glass - one of the rarest and most important collections of mediaeval stained glass windows in the world - was brought to England by a local landowner who had found it in a Belgium monastery which had fallen into disrepair after the Napoleonic wars. The landowner, in turn, sold the glass to the cathedral for £100. The glass has recently been cleaned and restored.

The Close, Lichfield WS13 7LD

- **Fradley Junction** is a popular place to stop and is close to a nature reserve. There are information boards telling the story of the canal. It can become very crowded at the weekend in summer, making navigation through it quite difficult.

THE FORTH & CLYDE CANAL

Opened in 1790, this canal enabled seagoing vessels to travel between the Firth of Forth and the Firth of Clyde across the centre of Scotland. The canal is 35 miles long and runs from Grangemouth in the east (where it meets the River Carron and is thereby connected to the River Forth) to Bowling in the west (where it meets the River Clyde). The canal has 39 large locks (68 feet long by 20 feet wide) capable of accommodating small seagoing vessels.

The Forth & Clyde and Union Canals used to be linked by a staircase of 11 locks. These were dismantled in 1933, leaving the Forth & Clyde isolated from everything except the rivers at either end. However, as part of the millennium celebrations, National Lottery funds were used to build the Falkirk Wheel which, by lifting or lowering boats from one canal to the other, has connected the two canals once again and opened up a 69 mile waterway route running from west to east coast.

The Wheel raises boats 79 feet onto an aqueduct that leads to a pair of locks connecting to the Union Canal which is another 36 feet higher. These locks have iron hooks instead of mooring bollards, and handspikes are needed to operate the paddle gear.

The construction of 330 yards of new canal and two new locks has enabled the Port Dundas branch in Glasgow to be reconnected from Stockingfield Junction to Pinkston Basin.

Locks and lift bridges on the Forth & Clyde are manned by Scottish Canals staff. An excellent guide to boating on this canal can be downloaded here:

https://www.scottishcanals.co.uk/wp-content/uploads/2015/05/ Scottish-Canals-Lowlands-Skippers-Guide-WEB-May-16.pdf

In passing: things to see and do

Places of note:

- **McMonagles** is a fish & chip restaurant on a boat which advertises itself as the world's first sail-through takeaway.
  Argyll Road, Clydebank G81 1QA
- **The Kelvin Aqueduct** which, unsurprisingly, carries the canal over the River Kelvin, opened in 1790 and is 445 feet long. Made of stone, it was the largest of its kind in Europe when it was built.

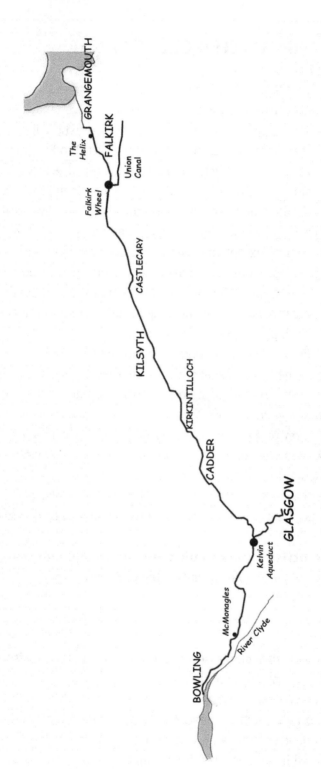

FORTH & CLYDE CANAL

- **The Falkirk Wheel** is worth visiting even if you don't want to go through it.
- **The Helix.** Between Falkirk and Grangemouth, this lottery funded project has transformed under-used land into a thriving urban green space including a performance area, a large lagoon with facilities for watersports, play areas, walks and cycleways. It also has ¾ million trees and various works of art including the world's largest equine statues - two silver Kelpie heads, 100 feet high.
  http://www.thehelix.co.uk/

Places to visit:
- **Cadder Parish Church.** There has been a church on this site since the 12th century. This church was built in 1825. Its particular interest lies in the watch house and mort-safe in the churchyard. At the time the church was built, body-snatching was common (the bodies being sold to hospitals and doctors for dissection and experimentation). The iron mort-safe - so heavy that it needed several men to lift it - would be left over a new grave for several days to prevent its desecration, while relatives and church officers kept watch from the watch house.
  Cadder Road, Bishopbriggs G64 3QA
- **The Auld Kirk Museum, Kirkintilloch,** has an exhibition of some 13,000 objects, dating from Roman times to the 20th century, and reflecting the everyday life of the people of East Dunbartonshire. The kirk itself was built in 1644.
  11, Cowgate, Kirkintilloch G66 1AB.

THE GRAND UNION CANAL

The main line of the Grand Union starts in Birmingham (where it meets the BCN) and ends at Brentford in West London (where it meets the Thames), making it the longest canal in the UK, covering 137 miles, with a total of 166 locks. Formed in 1929 from an amalgamation of several smaller canals, it has branches (or 'arms') to Leicester, Slough, Aylesbury, Wendover, Northampton and elsewhere.

At various points along its route, the canal links with the BCN, the Birmingham & Fazeley Canal, the Oxford Canal, the Trent & Mersey Canal, the Stratford-upon-Avon Canal and the Lee Navigation as well as the River Thames, the River Nene and the River Soar. Together with the River Thames and the Oxford Canal, the Grand Union main line forms part of the Thames Ring.

During the Second World War, the Grand Union was an important route for transporting coal and other essentials from Birmingham to London. A boat crew usually consisted of three women and the experiences of one such crew are recorded in Susan Wolfitt's book *Idle Women*.

In order to describe this very long canal, we have - somewhat arbitrarily - divided it into three sections:

1. The northern section running from the junction with the BCN in Birmingham to Gayton Junction, and including the Leicester Line and the Northampton, Welford and Market Harborough Arms.

2. The central section running from Gayton Junction, just north of the Blisworth Tunnel, to Bulbourn, just south of the Marsworth Locks and including the Aylesbury and Wendover Arms.

3. The southern section running from Bulbourn, just south of the Wendover Arm, to Brentford and the junction with the River Thames, and including the Slough and Paddington Arms and the Regent's and Hertford Union Canals.

THE NORTHERN SECTION

The Grand Union Canal begins at Warwick Bar in Birmingham and almost immediately passes through six locks. There is a flight of five locks at Knowle. Once past Kingswood Junction, where a short spur leads to the Stratford-upon-Avon Canal, the canal goes through the 433 yard long Shrewley Tunnel. In many canal tunnels with no towpaths, the horse would have to be led over the top to meet up with the boat at the other end, but Shrewley was built with a separate tunnel for the horses.

Shortly after the tunnel you come to the 21 locks that make up the Hatton Flight. The first 11 locks are tightly spaced but the remaining ten have more room between them. Nicknamed 'the stairway to heaven' these locks have hydraulic paddle gear which makes them less hard work, but they can be slow.

The canal travels through Warwick and Leamington Spa, being carried on aqueducts over the River Avon and what was the Great Western Railway. After a series of single locks, there is a flight of four at Bascoted, the top two of which form a staircase. This is quickly followed by the Stockton Flight of 10 locks, often known as 'the Itchington Ten' because of the location of the bottom lock close to the village of Long Itchington.

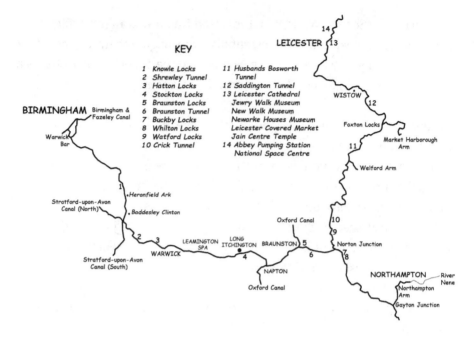

KEY

1 Knowle Locks	11 Husbands Bosworth Tunnel
2 Shrewley Tunnel	12 Saddington Tunnel
3 Hatton Locks	13 Leicester Cathedral
4 Stockton Locks	Jewry Walk Museum
5 Braunston Locks	New Walk Museum
6 Braunston Tunnel	Newarke Houses Museum
7 Buckby Locks	Leicester Covered Market
8 Whilton Locks	Jain Centre Temple
9 Watford Locks	14 Abbey Pumping Station
10 Crick Tunnel	National Space Centre

At Napton, the Grand Union meets the Oxford Canal and, for the next five miles, until Braunston is reached, the two become a single waterway. At Braunston, the Oxford branches off northwards and the Grand Union goes through the Braunston Flight of six locks before passing through the 2040 yard Braunston Tunnel. Shortly after the end of the tunnel, the Leicester Arm branches off at Norton Junction. Braunston Tunnel has an S bend in the middle so it's impossible to see from one end to the other. For over sixty years, until the mid 1930s, boats were guided through by steam tugs starting at hourly intervals from alternate ends.

After Norton Junction, the main line continues through the Buckby and Whilton Locks (seven in total) and then travels through a lockless section of just over 12 miles to Gayton Junction, where the Northampton Branch leaves it.

The Leicester Line

Running northwards between Norton Junction and Leicester where it joins the River Soar, this arm is about 41 miles long. On its route it goes through the Watford Locks (a flight of seven, four of which form a staircase), the 1,528 yard long Crick Tunnel, the 1,166 yard long Husbands Bosworth Tunnel, the Foxton Locks (consisting of two staircases of five locks each, with a passing place in the middle) and the 957 yard long Saddingworth Tunnel. The Foxton Locks, built in 1812, form the largest set of staircase locks in Britain.

In total, the Leicester line has 41 locks. Much of it, including its two arms, runs through open farmland. Together with the River Soar Navigation, River Trent, Trent & Mersey Canal, Coventry Canal and North Oxford Canal, the Leicester Line forms the Leicester Ring. It has two arms, the 1½ mile long Welford Arm, which has one lock and leads to the pretty village of Welford, and the 5½ mile long Market Harborough Arm which branches off at Foxton Junction and has no locks.

The Northampton Arm
This canal is only 4¾ miles long but has 17 locks. It runs from Gayton Junction into the centre of Northampton where it joins the navigable River Nene. Its route is mostly rural.

In passing: things to see and do
Places of note:
- **Norton Junction.** The toll house dates back to 1914 and there are two Victorian cottages.
- **Foxton Locks** have side ponds with reed beds, where you can often see herons and, sometimes, water voles.

Places to visit on the main line:
- **Birmingham.** For places to visit close to the start of this canal, see the listing for the Birmingham & Fazeley Canal.
- **Heronfield Ark Animal Sanctuary** is a rescue centre for small breeds & wildlife.
  Warwick Road, Heronfield, Knowle B93 0EE
  http://www.heronfieldark.org.uk/index.html
- **Baddesley Clinton** is a Tudor, timber-framed manor house, owned by the National Trust, with a moat, walled gardens, and Elizabethan interiors with priest's holes. St. Michael's Church, which shares a lot of history with the house, is a few hundred yards away.
  Rising Lane, Knowle B93 0DQ
- **Warwick Castle.** Originally built by William the Conqueror in 1068, the present mediaeval castle is said to be the finest in England.

Warwick CV34 4QU

https://www.warwick-castle.com/

- **The Collegiate Church of St. Mary, Warwick,** is one of England's most magnificent parish churches. The crypt (which houses a rare mediaeval ducking stool) is part of the original church, built in 1123. The chancel, vestry and chapter house date from the 14th century. The 15th century Beauchamp chapel has some superb stained glass and houses the tomb of Elizabeth I's favourite, Robert Dudley. In the north transept is the Warwickshire Regimental Chapel, where its regimental colours are displayed. The tower, which is 174 feet tall, was built in 1704 to replace one which was destroyed by fire ten years earlier.

  Old Square, Warwick CV34 4QU

  http://www.stmaryswarwick.org.uk/

- **Long Itchington** has half timbered houses, including one in which Elizabeth I is said to have stayed. The Manor House dates from the 15th century. The village has three other claims to fame - it was the birthplace of St. Wulfstan (died 1095), at the time of the Domesday Book it was 20 times bigger than Birmingham, and in 1898 a large fossil of an ichthyosaurus (now in the Natural History Museum in London) was found in a quarry lying between Long Itchington and the neighbouring village of Stockton.

  http://www.longitchington.org.uk/our-village/history/

- **Holy Trinity Church, Long Itchington.** Built in the 13th century, it has some interesting mediaeval carvings and one of the oldest rood screens in the country, dating from the 14th century.

  Church Road, Long Itchington CV47 9PN

Places to visit on the Leicester Line:

- **The inclined plane boat lift.** The remnants of this lift are to be found next to the Foxton Locks. Built in 1900, it was part of a scheme to create a wide-beam canal route which would speed up the passage of boats and allow for increased traffic. However, although the lift greatly reduced the passage time (12 minutes rather than 45) and saved a huge amount of water, there were problems - such as the lift not working at night, although the boats did. In the end, the proposed widening of the Watford Locks didn't happen and the lift was declared redundant in 1911. Enough remains to be interesting, and there is a good view from the top.

- **The Foxton Canal Museum** is housed in the old boiler house of the inclined plane boat lift. It has working models of the lift as well as other displays.
Middle Lock, Market Harborough LE16 7RA
- **Harborough Museum** is housed in a former corset factory and has collections celebrating Market Harborough's history as a centre of trade and industry, including the Symington collection of historical corsets.
The Symington Building, Adam and Eve Street, Market Harborough LE16 7LT
http://www.harboroughmuseum.org.uk/
- **St. Wistan's Church, Wistow,** is a Norman church, said to have been built at the place where St. Wistan was murdered by his cousin.
Kibworth Road, Wistow LE8 0QF
- **Wistow Maize Maze** is one of the largest in the country, covering some 8 acres, with 10 foot high bridges and viewing towers. The maze is redesigned every year and is open from mid July to mid September.
Kibworth Road, Wistow LE8 0QF
- **Wiston-le-Dale Model Village, Wistow.** Situated in a walled garden, the village has over 75 buildings including a castle, mill, church, town hall, shops, houses and cottages, together with a railway, canal and miniature trees and flowering plants.
Wistow Rural Centre, Wistow Road, Wistow LE8 0QF
- **Leicester Cathedral.** Built originally in the late 11th century, much of what is visible today is the result of later additions and restoration. The body of Richard III was reburied in the cathedral in 2015.
Peacock Lane, Leicester LE1 5DE
- **The New Walk Museum & Art Gallery, Leicester,** has galleries including Arts and Crafts, Picasso ceramics, German expressionism, Victorian art and ancient Egypt.
53 New Walk, Leicester LE1 7EA
- **The Jewry Wall Museum, Leicester,** has displays ranging from ancient stone tools to mediaeval decorated tiles, while the grounds contain the 2nd century Jewry Wall and part of the Roman public baths - one of the tallest pieces of Roman masonry in the country.
156-160 St. Nicholas Circle, Leicester LE1 4LB

- **Newarke Houses Museum, Leicester,** tells the social history of Leicester and includes a 1950s street scene, the museum of the Royal Leicestershire Regiment, and a collection of toys from Tudor times to the present day, together with a play area where children can try different games.
  The Newarke, Leicester, LE2 7BY
- **Leicester Covered Markets** is one of the largest in Europe.
  2-4 Market Place South, Leicester LE1 5HQ
  http://www.leicestermarket.co.uk/
- **Jain Centre Temple** was the first Jain temple to be built in the West.
  32 Oxford Street, Leicester LE1 5XU
- **Abbey Pumping Station** is Leicester's Museum of Science and Technology, and houses exhibitions on light and optics, historic transport and public health.
  Corporation Road, Leicester LE4 5PX
- **The National Space Centre, Leicester,** has six interactive galleries, the UK's largest planetarium, a 3D simulator experience and a 138 foot high rocket tower.
  Exploration Drive, Leicester LE4 5NS
  http://spacecentre.co.uk/

THE CENTRAL SECTION

Less than two miles past Gayton Junction, the canal reaches the Blisworth Tunnel (3056 yards long and the third longest canal tunnel in Britain) and, very shortly after that, the Stoke Bruerne Flight of seven locks. There is then a flat section of some 5¾ miles until you reach Cosgrove with its one lock followed by two aqueducts - the 'Iron Trunk' Aqueduct over the River Ouse and then the Grafton Street Aqueduct at New Bradwell.

The canal snakes around the top and eastern outskirts of Milton Keynes to reach Fenny Stratford Lock which not only is the smallest lock on the canal (having a drop of just one foot), but has a swing bridge across it. This is followed by some scattered locks (including a flight of three at Soulbury) before the canal reaches Leighton Buzzard and continues on past the villages of Slapton, Horton and Cheddington, this section being commonly known as 'the Slapton fields'. After a series of single locks, the Aylesbury Arm branches off and the main line enters the Marsworth Flight of seven locks, at the top of which, the short Wendover Arm branches off under a bridge.

1 Northampton Arm

Gayton Junction

BLISWORTH

COSGROVE

MILTON KEYNES

SLAPTON

TRING

Aylesbury Arm   Wendover Arm

KEY

1 Northampton Museum & Art Gallery
2 Northampton Ironstone Railway
3 Blisworth Tunnel
4 Stoke Bruerne Brick Pits Nature Reserve
   Stoke Bruerne Canal Museum
   Rookery Open Farm
5 Stoke Bruerne Locks
6 Cosgrove Iron Trunk Aqueduct
7 Grafton Street Aqueduct
8 Willen Lake & St. Mary Magdalene Church
9 Bletchley Park
10 All Saints Church, Leighton Buzzard
11 Pitstone Windmill
12 Bucks County Museum
13 Marsworth Locks

The Aylesbury Arm

This arm is about 6¼ miles long and has sixteen locks, of which the first two after Marsworth Junction form a staircase. It mostly travels through open farmland and ends at Aylesbury Canal Basin, just a short walk from the town centre. You will need a CRT key to open locks 7, 9, 10, 11 and 15 - make sure you hire company has supplied you with one.

The Wendover Arm

This is navigable for only about a mile. It has two bridges but no locks.

In passing: things to see and do

Places of note:

- **The Iron Trunk Aqueduct** between Cosgrove and Wolverton is a scheduled ancient monument which traverses the River Ouse. Built in 1811, it succeeded a short-lived flight of locks which went down to the river and up again. These, in their turn, had replaced a stone aqueduct that collapsed in 1808. Just before the aqueduct is reached, the canal passes the grounds of Cosgrove Hall, an 18th century house which was badly damaged by fire in 2016. Visible from the canal are the ruins of a Roman bath house which have been excavated in its grounds.

- **The Grafton Street Aqueduct, New Bradwell,** was built in 1991 and was the first new aqueduct to be built on the Grand Union canal in over 100 years.

Places to visit:

- **Northampton Museum & Art Gallery.** Collections on display include pottery, porcelain, glassware, archaeology, European paintings spanning four centuries, leathercraft - and the world's largest collection of footwear. 4 - 6 Guildhall Road, Northampton NN1 1DP
- **Northampton Ironstone Railway Trust** is a 1½ mile long heritage line mainly dedicated to freight working but with rides available in a variety of vehicles including a converted brake van.
  Hunsbury Hill Road, Camp Hill NN4 9UW
  http://www.nirt.co.uk/
- **Stoke Bruerne Brick Pits Nature Reserve** lies between Blisworth Tunnel and the Stoke Bruerne Locks. Inhabitants include redwings, barn owls, reed warblers and reed buntings, as well as frogs, toads and newts.
  Stoke Bruerne NN12 7SY
- **Stoke Bruerne Canal Museum,** which is housed in an 1840s corn mill, tells the story of Britain's inland waterways and the people who worked on them. The exhibits include a number of working models.
  3 Bridge Road, Stoke Bruerne NN12 7SE (next to the top lock)
- **Rookery Open Farm** is aimed specifically at children.
  Rookery Lane, Stoke Bruerne NN12 7SJ
  http://www.rookeryopenfarm.com
- **Willen Lake** is a popular stop for some rare migrating bird species. In the adjoining park is a Buddhist peace pagoda, built in 1980 and the first of its kind to be built in the West.
  Brickhill Street, Milton Keynes MK15 0DS
- **St. Mary Magdalene Church, Willen,** is just north of Willen Lake. A grade I listed building, it was designed in the late 17th century by Robert Hooke, Curator of Experiments at the Royal Society and City Surveyor for reconstruction after the Great Fire of London.
  Milton Road, Willen Village MK15 9AB
- **Bletchley Park,** where the British broke the German Enigma code, thus playing an important part in the Allied victory in WWII, is quite close to the Fenny Stratford Lock. It is now open to the public as the National Museum of Computing.
  The Mansion, Bletchley Park, Sherwood Drive, Bletchley MK3 6EB
  https://www.bletchleypark.org.uk/

- **All Saints Church, Leighton Buzzard,** dates from the 13th century and boasts, among other things, late 14th century misericords, some fine windows, a 13th century eagle lectern and a font which probably came from an earlier church on this site. It was restored in the 1980s after a fire.

  Church Square, Leighton Buzzard LU7 1AE

  http://www.allsaintslb.org.uk/
- **Pitstone Windmill** is a National Trust property and probably dates to the early 17th century, making it one of the oldest post mills in Britain. It is surrounded by 5,000 acres of woodland and parkland, and there is a visitor centre.

  Ivinghoe, Pitstone, Leighton Buzzard LU7 9ER
- **The Bucks County Museum** holds an important costume and textile collection amounting to nearly 10,000 items. There are also collections of archaeology, art, coins, wildlife and geology, many of the exhibits relating to the local area, and the museum is home to the Roald Dahl Children's Gallery.

  Church Street, Aylesbury HP20 2QP

  http://www.buckscountymuseum.org/museum/

THE SOUTHERN SECTION

Once through the Marsworth Locks, there is a flat section of just over three miles past Tring, on the summit of the Chiltern hills, before the locks begin again. Just before Berkhamsted, Locks 49 (Northchurch) to 51 (Gas Lock 1) are locked and unavailable between 9pm and 8am daily, while Lock 53 (Berkhamsted) and Bridge 147 (Winkwell Swing Bridge at Bourne End) require a CRT key to open them.

Soon after passing Abbots Langley (birthplace of the only English Pope, Adrian IV) the canal goes through Cassiobury Park, an area of 190 acres, with a nature trail and a lot of facilities for children.

Eventually, having gone through 44 locks since leaving Tring, Cowley Lock is reached, which heralds a flat section of just over six miles before the eight locks of the Hanwell Flight. Four more locks and the canal reaches Brentford in West London, where it joins the River Thames. These final twelve locks need a CRT key to open them.

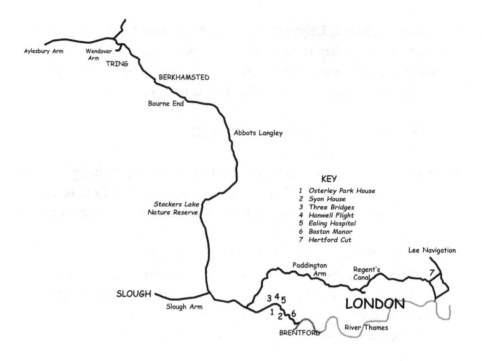

KEY

1 Osterley Park House
2 Syon House
3 Three Bridges
4 Hanwell Flight
5 Ealing Hospital
6 Boston Manor
7 Hertford Cut

The Slough Arm

Leaving the Grand Union just before Uxbridge, at Cowley Peachey Junction, the Slough Arm travels 5 miles, with no locks, and a short aqueduct over the River Frays, into the centre of Slough. The first part is semi-rural.

The Paddington Arm, the Regent's Canal and the Hertford Union Canal

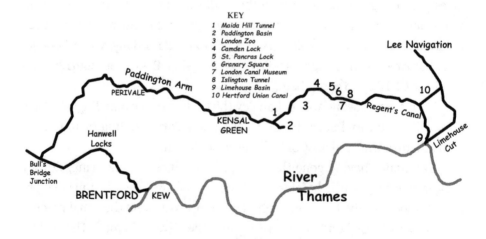

KEY

1 Maida Hill Tunnel
2 Paddington Basin
3 London Zoo
4 Camden Lock
5 St. Pancras Lock
6 Granary Square
7 London Canal Museum
8 Islington Tunnel
9 Limehouse Basin
10 Hertford Union Canal

At Bulls Bridge, 3¼ miles after the Slough Arm branches off, the Paddington Arm leaves the main line and runs 12 miles to end at the Paddington Basin, having joined the Regent's Canal shortly before at Little Venice. The Paddington Arm is 13½ miles long and has no locks. Between Bridges 11 and 10 it is carried by two consecutive aqueducts over the River Brent and the North Circular Road. It forms part of a short cruising ring, going past the Houses of Parliament on the River Thames and joining the Grand Union Canal at Brentford. However, hired narrow boats are not allowed onto this part of the Thames and, in any case, this section should only be attempted by experienced boaters as the Thames is a tidal waterway and very busy.

The Regent's Canal runs for 8½ miles from Little Venice (where it meets the Paddington Arm) to Limehouse Basin (where it meets the Limehouse Cut). Shortly after the Little Venice junction, it runs through the 272 yard long Maida Hill Tunnel and then curves around the top of London Zoo to Camden Town and the area known as 'Camden Lock' which, in fact, comprises three locks. A little over half a mile later, the canal goes through Islington Tunnel, which is 960 yards long. After another three miles and four locks, the Hertford Union Canal branches off and the Regent's Canal then continues for a little under two miles, and through four more locks, to Limehouse Basin.

Also known as Duckett's Cut after its designer, the Hertford Union Canal is a stretch of about a mile that connects the Regent's Canal to the Lee Navigation, providing a shortcut from the Regent's Canal to the River Lee, avoiding the River Thames. It runs beside the pleasant open spaces of Hackney's Victoria Park, which has lakes, sculptures, a deer enclosure and even a Chinese pagoda. From the point at which the canal joins the Lee Navigation, you can see London's Olympic Stadium.

In passing: things to see and do
Places of note on the main line:
- **At Berkhamsted** there is a large Canadian totem pole next to the canal.
- **Three Bridges** is actually a system of just two bridges designed by Isambard Kingdom Brunel to allow the Great Western & Brentford Railway to be crossed by an aqueduct carrying the Grand Junction Canal which, itself, is crossed by a road bridge (Windmill Lane). The bridges, completed in 1859, are now a scheduled ancient monument.

- **The Hanwell Flight** of six locks is a scheduled ancient monument.
- **Ealing Hospital.** Next to the Hanwell Flight is the outer wall of what was London's first county 'pauper and lunatic asylum' and which now forms part of Ealing Hospital. Between Locks 93 and 94 you can see a blocked up arch which was originally the entrance to the hospital for patients who were brought by boat.

Places to visit from the main line:
- **Tring** is a pretty market town
- **Tring Natural History Museum.** Once the private museum of the 2nd Baron Rothschild, this is now a branch of the Natural History Museum and houses one of the finest collections of stuffed mammals, birds, reptiles and insects in the United Kingdom.
  The Walter Rothschild Building, Akeman Street, Tring HP23 6AP
  http://www.nhm.ac.uk/visit/tring.html
- **Berkhamsted** is a historic market town and was the birthplace of the author Graham Greene. The local council has devised several walks with audio guides that can be downloaded here:
  http://www.berkhamstedtowncouncil.gov.uk/town-guide.html
  There is also a 'Graham Greene' walk, around the places that influenced his life and work, with a map that can be downloaded from here:
  http://grahamgreenebt.org/gg-trail/
- **Berkhamsted Castle.** The substantial remains of an important motte and bailey castle dating from the 11th-13th centuries, with surrounding walls, ditches and earthworks. Close to Lock 53.
- **St. Peter's Church, Berkhamsted.** Built at the beginning of the 13th century and restored in the 19th, it has windows dating from the 13th and 14th centuries as well as Victorian stained glass, 14th century brasses, a coffin top tomb dating from about 1200 and, in the churchyard, a yew tree that is probably about 350 years old.
  Church Lane, Berkhamsted HP4 2AX
- **Stocker's Lake Nature Reserve, Maple Cross.** A large former gravel pit (which provided the gravel for the construction of the original Wembley stadium), surrounded by smaller lakes, wet woodland and reedbeds. At various times of the year you can see shoveler and goldeneye ducks, kingfishers, grey herons, common terns, and - occasionally - smew, red-

crested pochard, osprey, goosander and others. Close to Lock 83.
http://www.wildfuture.co.uk/index.php/stockers-lake-hertfordshire

- **Osterley Park House** is a National Trust property, originally built as a manor house in the 1570s and extensively remodelled in the late 18th century by Robert Adam. It has Georgian furniture, paintings and tapestries, and is surrounded by parkland, with a summer house, designed by Adam, containing lemon trees and scented shrubs.
  Jersey Road, Isleworth TW7 4RB
- **Syon House** is the home of the Duke of Northumberland. Built in the 16th century on the site of the mediaeval Syon Abbey, it has magnificent state apartments, bedrooms used by the young Princess Victoria and her mother, a spectacular conservatory and 40 acres of gardens.
  Syon Park, Brentford TW8 8JF
  http://www.syonpark.co.uk/
- **Boston Manor House,** Park and Nature Trail. Only part of this semi-restored Jacobean Manor House is open to the public. The nature trail includes part of the canal towpath.
- **The Royal Botanic Gardens,** Kew, houses the largest and most diverse collection of plants and fungi in the world.
  http://www.kew.org/

Places of note on the Paddington Arm:
- **Bull's Bridge Junction** (the junction with the main line). The brick bridge was built in 1801 and is grade II listed. Nearby is a 19th century toll house.
- **Kensal Green Cemetery.** The south side borders the canal and the landing platforms can be seen where coffins used to be brought by hearse barges.

Places to visit on the Paddington Arm:
- **Perivale Wood** is one of the oldest nature reserves in Britain. Right next to the canal, it consists of 27 acres of oak woodland - a remnant of the ancient Middlesex Forest.
  Sunley Gardens, Perivale UB6 7PE
- **Kensal Green Cemetery.** Opened in 1833, it consists of 72 acres, including two conservation areas, and is home to 33 species of bird and other wildlife. The list of those buried here reads like a Who's Who of actors,

sportsmen, scientists, politicians, musicians, soldiers, doctors, writers, lawyers, explorers, engineers and artists and includes Isambard Kingdom Brunel, Wilkie Collins, William Makepeace Thackeray, Anthony Trollope and Terence Rattigan as well as Blondin, the French acrobat who crossed Niagara Falls on a tightrope.
Harrow Road, London W10 4RA

Places of note on the Regent's Canal:
- **At Bridge 27** (by Hampstead Road Lock) the River Fleet is carried across the canal by a large pipe on the underside of the bridge!
- **Ramps** leading from the canal to the towpath between Camden Locks and St. Pancras Lock were put there to help horses that had fallen in to return to dry land.
- **The 1870s water tower** next to St. Pancras lock no longer stands where it was originally built - it had to be moved when the Eurostar rail tracks were laid.

Places to visit from the Regent's Canal:
- **The London Zoo.** The world's oldest scientific zoo was set up for research in 1828 and was opened to the public 19 years later. It houses over 17,000 creatures, consisting of 756 different species. The canal passes directly by the aviary.
London NW1 4RY
https://www.zsl.org/zsl-london-zoo
- **The castellated lock keeper's cottage at Hampstead Road Lock** is now a coffee shop but also houses an interesting display on the history of the canal.
- **Camden Market,** running alongside the three Camden Locks, has over 1000 shops and stalls selling fashion, music, art, crafts, food and antiques. Camden Lock Place, London NW1 8AL
- **Granary Square.** A huge public square with over 1000 choreographed fountains, this was originally a canal basin where boats unloaded their freight.
Kings Cross, London N1C 4AA
- **Word on the Water** is London's only floating bookshop. Housed in a 1920s Dutch barge, it is to be found next to Granary Square and has been

voted the world's 9th most interesting independent bookshop!
http://www.uklisting.net/biz/wordonthewater
- **The London Canal Museum, Battlebridge Basin.** Housed in a Victorian ice warehouse, the museum was opened in 1992 and has exhibits covering all aspects of the UK's waterways.
12-13 New Wharf Road, Kings Cross N1 9RT
http://www.canalmuseum.org.uk/

Places of note on the Hertford Union Canal:
- **Lock no. 1 (Top Lock).** The cast iron footbridge that passes over the tail of the lock is grade II listed, as is one of the Lock Cottages (no. 3). The bottom gates of the lock have rare cast iron balance beams.

THE HUDDERSFIELD BROAD CANAL

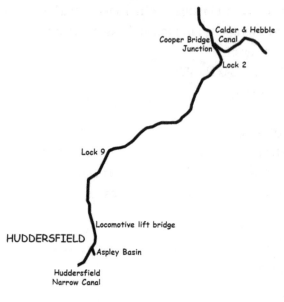

Also known as Sir John Ramsden's Canal after a local landowner who supported its construction, this West Yorkshire canal is only 3¾ miles long but has nine wide locks. Completed in 1776, it provides a link between the Calder & Hebble Navigation (which it meets at Cooper Bridge Junction) and the Huddersfield Narrow Canal (which it meets just beyond Aspley Basin in Huddersfield). The locks are quite short, so if your boat is longer than about 57 feet, you won't be able to use this canal.

In passing: things to see

- **Lock 1.** Coming very shortly after the junction, this is grade II listed, as is the adjacent 19th century lock keeper's cottage.
- **An 18th century stone warehouse** is to be seen just above Lock 2 (Colne Bridge Lock).
- **The arched bridge immediately following Lock 2** was built in 1775 and has a date stone to that effect.
- **The Locomotive Lift Bridge** was installed in 1865 and converted to electrical operation in 2002. Nearby is an octagonal chimney, over 100 feet tall, that was originally part of a cotton spinning mill built in 1872.
- **Two canal warehouses** just before Aspley Basin were built around the same time as the canal. The second of these (just after Wakefield Road Bridge) is grade II* listed.

For places to visit in Huddersfield, see the next section (Huddersfield Narrow Canal).

THE HUDDERSFIELD NARROW CANAL

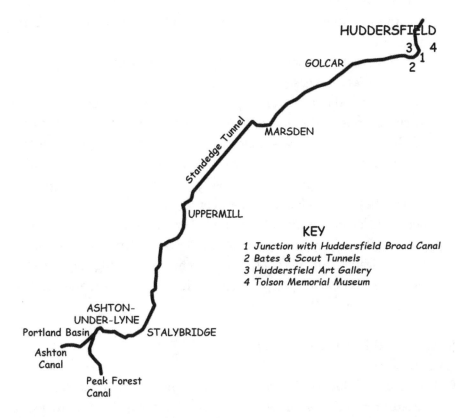

KEY

1 Junction with Huddersfield Broad Canal
2 Bates & Scout Tunnels
3 Huddersfield Art Gallery
4 Tolson Memorial Museum

Approximately 19½ miles long, this canal runs from close to the Aspley Basin in Huddersfield (where it meets the Huddersfield Broad Canal) to Whitelands Basin in Ashton-Under-Lyne, where it meets the Ashton and the Peak Forest Canals. Completed in 1811, it crosses the Pennines, travelling through glorious moorland and passing through 74 locks and three tunnels. Two of these - the Bates Tunnel and the Scout Tunnel - are relatively short (100 yards and 205 yards respectively). However, the third, the Standedge Tunnel, is 5700 yards long - that's nearly 3¼ miles - which makes it the longest canal tunnel in the UK.

Locks 21W and 22W at Uppermill (the 11th & 12th locks west of the Standedge Tunnel) are unevenly shaped and narrow and require careful manoeuvring, while a windlass and handcuff key are needed to operate Locks 1W and 2W, at the Ashton end of the canal.

Boats travelling through the Standedge Tunnel have to book ahead, since they have to be accompanied by a trained CRT 'chaperone'. Similarly, some of the locks require that CRT staff assist. Information regarding the Tunnel is available here:

https://canalrivertrust.org.uk/media/library/8217-standedge-boaters-guidelines.pdf

or you can contact the relevant office by 'phone on 0303 040 4040 or by email on *enquiries.manchesterpennine@canalrivertrust.org.uk*

In 2001, when the canal was reopened after nearly 40 years, there was a second, short tunnel at the Huddersfield end constructed, with an additional lock, to allow the canal to pass under the Sellers Engineering site. But this company moved in 2011 so the tunnel has been opened up and the canal brought back up to the surface. Boats now go straight through Lock 3E, and another lock has been built at the far end of the site.

Both Huddersfield Canals, Broad and Narrow, form part of the South Pennine Ring (together with the Ashton and Rochdale Canals and the Calder & Hebble Navigation) and part of the Outer Pennine Ring (together with the Bridgewater, Leeds & Liverpool, Ashton and Rochdale Canals, and the Aire & Calder and Calder & Hebble Navigations).

In passing: things to see and do

Places of note:

- **University of Huddersfield** campus flanks the start of the canal.
- **The summit of the canal** comes after the Marsden flight of twelve locks. This is the highest stretch of canal in Britain. There should be time for you to admire the view, since this is where you moor to await your passage through the Standedge Tunnel.
- **The Standedge Tunnel,** at 5700 yards long, is the longest canal tunnel in the United Kingdom. It is also the highest, being 645 feet above sea level. Much of it is brick lined but about a third shows the natural rock surface.

Places to visit:

- **Huddersfield Art Gallery** has works by L.S. Lowry, Francis Bacon and Henry Moore as well as by significant local artists.
  Princess Street, Huddersfield HD1 2SU
- **Tolson Memorial Museum.** The collections cover transport (including Britain's rarest car, manufactured locally for only five years in the early 20th century), textiles, birds, WWI, musical instruments, and 19th century

law-enforcement and law-breaking.
Wakefield Road, Dalton HD5 8DJ

- **Colne Valley Museum, Golcar.** Housed in three converted 19th century weavers' cottages, the museum gives an insight into the life of weavers in the early 1850s and includes a clog maker's workshop, a handloom chamber, a spinning room, kitchen and living rooms.
Cliffe Ash, Golcar HD7 4PY
http://www.colnevalleymuseum.org.uk/
- **The Mikron Theatre Company** is a group of players who tour the waterways on a narrowboat, bringing theatre to waterside pubs and village halls. They also perform at the Mechanics Institute, Marsden, where they are based.
https://www.mikron.org.uk/
- **St. Bartholomew's Church, Marsden.** Built in 1911, it has been described as "the Cathedral of the Colne Valley". It has a fine carved screen and reredos, a carved alabaster representation of the Last Supper, Carrara marble mosaics and stained glass windows designed by many different artists.
Church Lane, Marsden HD7 6DJ
- **Marsden Visitor Centre** is next to the Standedge Tunnel and has information and audio-visuals about the canal and the tunnel and their 200 years of history.
Waters Road, Marsden HD7 6NQ
- **Saddleworth Museum & Art Gallery.** The collections, which include geology, archaeology, costume and domestic life, tell the story of the people, events and history of Saddleworth and include a walk-in Victorian parlour and activity areas for children.
High Street, Uppermill OL3 6HS
http://www.saddleworthmuseum.co.uk
- **The Astley Cheetham Art Gallery, Stalybridge,** includes works by 15th century Italian masters and British artists of the 19th and 20th centuries.
Trinity Street, Stalybridge SK15 2BN
http://www.tameside.gov.uk/astleycheetham
- **Portland Basin Museum.** Close to the junction with the Ashton Canal, this museum is housed in a restored 19th century warehouse. The exhibits include local crafts and a 1920s street as well as items relating to the area's industrial heritage.
1 Portland Place, Ashton-under-Lyne OL7 0QA

THE KENNET & AVON CANAL

Although always referred to as a canal, the Kennet & Avon is, strictly speaking, a navigation in that it shares part of its course with rivers - the Avon in the west and the Kennet in the east. The canal section is 57 miles long and was built between 1794 and 1810, but the whole waterway is 87 miles long. It has 105 locks, including several flights.

It passes through some beautiful scenery and several Sites of Special Scientific Interest including the Aldermaston Gravel Pits, Woolhampton, Thatcham Reed Beds, and Freeman's Marsh at Hungerford. Surveys along the length of the canal have recorded over 100 species of birds, including grey herons, reed buntings and kingfishers. Attempts have also been made to encourage water voles.

The canal is popular with fishermen since it contains bream, tench, roach, rudd, perch, gudgeon, pike and carp. However, if you want to fish, you need to obtain a licence from the local angling association.

For convenience (and to make the sketch maps a bit clearer) we have divided the canal into five sections:
1. from Bristol to Bathampton (14½ miles)
2. from Bathampton to Devizes (19 miles)
3. from Devizes to the Bruce Tunnel (18 miles)
4. from the Bruce Tunnel to Newbury (17½ miles)
5. from Newbury to Reading (18 miles)

1. FROM BRISTOL TO BATHAMPTON

The canal starts at Hanham Lock (Lock 1). Beyond this, to the west, the River Avon is tidal. Starting off from here, you can see the Clifton Suspension Bridge in the distance.

Hanham Lock itself is surrounded by trees and the canal passes through some beautiful woodland between here and Bath, as well as six locks which raise it 30 feet within 12 miles.

At Bath, the canal leaves the river and goes through the six locks of the Widcombe Flight which raise it another 60 feet. After this, there are no locks between here and Bathampton.

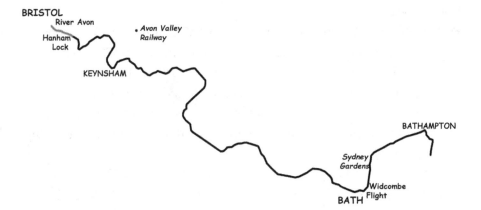

In passing: things to see and do

Places of note:

- **Widcombe Flight.** At the top of the flight is a cast iron footbridge, dating from around 1815, and the original lock keeper's cottage.
- **Lock 8/9 on the Widcombe Flight** is the result of Locks 8 & 9 being combined in 1976, as part of the canal restoration. It is now also known as Bath Deep Lock and is 19 feet 5 inches deep, making it one of the UK's deepest canal locks, second only to the Tuel Lane Lock on the Rochdale Canal, which is 3½ inches deeper.
- **Sydney Gardens.** As the canal heads north, in a large loop, following the course of the river, it passes through the oldest gardens in Bath, which were opened in 1795 . There is a very short tunnel at either end of the gardens. One of these, the Cleveland Tunnel, is 173 feet long and runs under Cleveland House, a grade II* listed building which used to be the headquarters of the Kennet & Avon Canal Company. The clerks in the offices would pass paperwork down to the passing boats via a trapdoor in the tunnel roof. There are also several ornate early 19th century cast iron bridges, some of which are listed structures.
- **The George Inn, Bathampton.** Just north of the canal in Mill Lane, Bathampton is the 17th century grade II listed inn where Viscount John Baptiste Du Barry died in 1778 after being wounded in the last legal duel in Britain. His ghost is said to haunt the inn.

Places to visit:

- **The SS Great Britain and the Dockyard Museum, Bristol.** Built of iron and powered by a 1000 horse power steam engine, the SS Great Britain was designed by Brunel and launched in 1843. At the time, it was the largest passenger ship that had been built and the first to use a screw propeller instead of conventional paddle wheels. It became the first iron steamer to cross the Atlantic. The Dockyard Museum covers the ship's long history.
  Great Western Dockyard, Gas Ferry Road, Bristol BS1 6TY
  http://www.ssgreatbritain.org/
- **The Avon Valley Railway** is a three mile long steam railway that crosses the canal twice.
  Bitton Station, Bath Road, Bitton BS30 6HD
  http://www.avonvalleyrailway.org/
- **Bath** is a beautiful Georgian city with numerous attractions including the Roman Baths, the Assembly Rooms and Bath Abbey which was founded in the 7th century and rebuilt in the 12th and 16th centuries
  https://visitbath.co.uk/
- **The Holburne Museum** is a grade I listed building housing a collection of fine and decorative art including porcelain, paintings and sculpture.
  Great Pulteney Street, Bathwick BA2 4DB
  http://www.holburne.org/
- **The Museum of East Asian Art** is the only UK museum dedicated solely to the arts of China, Japan, Korea and South East Asia. Displays include jade, ceramics, lacquer and metalware dating from about 5000BC to the 20th century.
  12 Bennett Street, Bath BA1 2QJ
  http://meaa.org.uk/
- **The Fashion Museum** is one of the top 10 costume museums in the world.
  Assembly Rooms, Bennett Street, Bath BA1 2QH
  https://www.fashionmuseum.co.uk/
- **The Museum of Bath Architecture** offers an insight into the planning and building of the Georgian city.
  The Countess of Huntingdon's Chapel, The Vineyards, The Paragon, Bath BA1 5NA
  http://museumofbatharchitecture.org.uk/

- **The Victoria Art Gallery**
  Bridge Street, Bath BA2 4AT
  https://www.victoriagal.org.uk/
- **The Bath Postal Museum**
  27 Northgate Street, Bath BA1 1AJ
  http://www.bathpostalmuseum.co.uk/
- **The Herschel Museum of Astronomy** is housed in the Georgian town house that was the home of the 18th-19th century astronomers William and Caroline Herschel.
  19 New King Street, Bath BA1 2BL
  http://herschelmuseum.org.uk/
- **The Jane Austen Centre** offers an insight into what it would be like to have lived in Regency times.
  40 Gay Street, Queen Square, Bath BA1 2NT
  https://www.janeausten.co.uk/
- **The Bath Medical Museum** has displays of photographs, medical instruments and documents relating to Bath's long history as a spa town.
  Royal National Hospital for Rheumatic Diseases, Upper Borough Walls, Bath BA1 1RL
  https://bathmedicalmuseum.org/
- **Bathampton Meadow** is a 22 acre site, close to the canal, with wet meadows and an oxbow lake where a wide variety of migratory birds can be seen including dunlin, ringed plovers, and green and common sandpipers, as well as sand martins, kingfishers, yellow wagtails, whinchats and hobbys.
- **St. Nicholas' Church, Bathampton.** Built in the 13th century, this is a grade II* listed building. Its tower was added in the 15th century and the church itself underwent some restoration during the 18th and 19th centuries.
  Mill Lane, Bathampton, BA2 6TU

2. FROM BATHAMPTON TO DEVIZES

The canal crosses the River Avon and the Wessex Main Line Railway on the Dundas Aqueduct, where the disused Somerset Coal Canal branches off towards Monkton Combe. The Coal Canal, which opened in 1805 and closed in 1904, was used to carry coal from the North Somerset coalfields to the

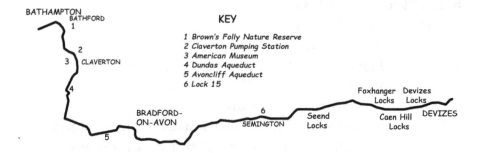

Kennet & Avon Canal and, at its peak, carried around 100,000 tons a year. At the Avoncliff Aqueduct, the canal once again crosses both river and railway. Care needs to be taken here with steering, since the canal takes a 90 degree turn to the right to get onto the aqueduct, and a 90 degree turn to the left to leave it.

The section of the canal between Bath and Bradford-on-Avon passes through some beautiful countryside and the towpath is very popular with cyclists. Pedestrians need to take care. This section also has quite a few swing bridges.

At Semington, the canal passes through two locks. It was from the first of these, Lock 15, that the disused Wilts & Berks Canal branched off to travel 52 miles across country, through Swindon and on to Abingdon in Oxfordshire, where it met the River Thames.

A little further on are the four Seend Locks and then comes the flight of 29 locks at Devizes. The first seven, the Foxhangers Locks, are spread over ¾ of a mile. They lead into the sixteen Caen Hill Locks and the final six Devizes Locks. Together, they raise the canal 237 feet in two miles. Because the hill is so steep, the Caen Hill Locks had to be built very close to each other and there was no space for the builders to put water pounds between them. So to store the water they need, there are large side ponds. A pump, installed at Foxhangers in 1996, is capable of returning 32 million litres of water to the top of the flight each day. Water conservation is very important and passage through the locks is overseen by lock keepers who may ask you to wait for a second boat to arrive so you can go up together. The locks cannot be used before 8am and boats have to be clear of the Caen Hill Flight before dusk. Passage through the locks takes about two and a half hours, so you need to plan carefully to ensure that you don't arrive too late in the day to get through.

Just beyond the top lock is Devizes Wharf from which, every Easter weekend since 1948, competitors in the Devizes to Westminster International Canoe Marathon have started off, heading for Westminster, 125 miles away. It usually takes the winners between 16 and 18 hours to complete the course.

In passing: places to visit

- **Brown's Folly Nature Reserve.** A 10 acre Site of Special Scientific Interest offering grasslands and ancient woodland with some spectacular views. Flora includes wild thyme, harebells, nine species of orchid (including the rare fly orchid), ferns and unusual plants such as Bath asparagus. The woodland is home to woodpeckers.
  Just south of Bathford.

- **Claverton Pumping Station.** This environmentally-friendly pumping station opened in 1813 and worked continuously until 1952, lifting 98,500 gallons an hour 48 feet to the Kennet & Avon Canal from the River Avon. After lying derelict for some years, it was restored by a group of volunteers and reopened in 1978. It is only open for a few days each year - for details see the website.
  Ferry Lane, Claverton BA2 7BH
  http://www.claverton.org/

- **The American Museum in Britain** has a wide range of exhibits including an exceptionally fine collection of quilts, a superb collection of maps from the 16th century and earlier, and an American heritage collection with Native American artefacts, Shaker furniture and much else. This is the only museum of its kind in Europe.
  Claverton Manor, Claverton Down BA2 7BD
  https://americanmuseum.org/

- **Bradford-on-Avon** is a pretty town set in a wooded valley, and it has many interesting buildings. The River Avon runs through the town and is crossed by an ancient nine arched bridge on which stands a small mediaeval chapel that was used as a prison in the 18th century.

- **Barton Farm Country Park.** Situated between the Avoncliff Aqueduct and Bradford-on-Avon, the park consists of 36 acres bordering the canal, and has a 14th century grade II* listed stone tithe barn which is 180 feet long, with two porches, massive wooden doors and a beamed roof.
  Pound Lane, Bradford-on-Avon BA15 1LF

- **Holy Trinity Church, Bradford-on-Avon,** is a beautiful Norman church, which has recently been restored.
  Church Street, Bradford-on-Avon BA15 1LW
- **St. Laurence's Church, Bradford-on-Avon,** is one of the best preserved Saxon churches in England.
  Church Street, Bradford-on-Avon BA15 1LQ
  http://www.greatenglishchurches.co.uk/html/bradford-on-avon.html
- **The Kennet & Avon Canal Museum.** Situated next to the top lock of the Devizes Flight, this museum has a wide range of artefacts illustrating the history of the canal.
  Couch Lane, Devizes SN10 1EB

3. FROM DEVIZES TO THE BRUCE TUNNEL

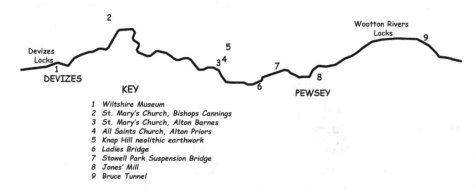

KEY
1 Wiltshire Museum
2 St. Mary's Church, Bishops Cannings
3 St. Mary's Church, Alton Barnes
4 All Saints Church, Alton Priors
5 Knap Hill neolithic earthwork
6 Ladies Bridge
7 Stowell Park Suspension Bridge
8 Jones' Mill
9 Bruce Tunnel

After the Devizes flight, you have a chance to recover, with 14 miles of canal through open countryside before the next lock at Wootton Rivers. Four spaced locks are followed by the short Bruce Tunnel. Other than the very short Bath Tunnels 1 & 2, this is the only tunnel on the Kennet & Avon. Opened in 1809, it is 502 yards long and was only made necessary by the fact that the landowner refused to allow a deep cut to be made through his land and insisted on a tunnel instead. He was Thomas Brudenell-Bruce, 1st Earl of Aylesbury, and the tunnel is named after him. It is a wide tunnel but has no towpath, so boatmen used to have to haul their boats through by means of chains that ran along its walls.

In passing: things to see and do

Places of note:

- **White horses.** There are several white horses carved into the chalk hillsides in this area. One of these can be seen from Alton Barnes and from several other points along the canal.
- **Ladies Bridge** (Bridge 120) stands out from the other canal bridges in the area since it is very ornate. It was designed by John Rennie in 1808 after the landowner made the building of such a bridge a condition for allowing the canal to go through his land.
- **Stowell Park Suspension Bridge** (Bridge 116) is also unusual. Built around 1845, it is a small iron suspension bridge and the only one of its kind still surviving.

Places to visit:

- **The Wiltshire Museum, Devizes,** has collections of archaeology, art and natural history illustrating the history of Wiltshire from Palaeolithic times to the present day and including important treasures from the time of Stonehenge.
  41 Long Street, Devizes SN10 1NS
  http://www.wiltshiremuseum.org.uk/
- **St. Mary's Church, Bishops Cannings,** is a grade I listed building dating from the 12th or 13th century, with some alterations made in the 14th and 15th centuries and some 19th century restoration. A 'confessional chair' or 'meditation pew' (a desk with a painted hand inscribed in Latin with various cautionary phrases) dates from the 15th century.
  Chandlers Lane, Bishops Cannings SN10 2LE
- **St. Mary's Church, Alton Barnes,** dates from Saxon times and has a yew tree in the churchyard which is thought to be 1700 years old. The nave roof dates from the 16th century. The red brick chancel, which was rebuilt in 1748, has 14th century windows while the window in the south chancel has stained glass by Lawrence Whistler. There is an 18th century triple decker pulpit, and the box pews and large font date from the Georgian period.
  Church Farm Lane, Alton Barnes SN8 4LE
- **All Saints Church, Alton Priors,** is a 12th century grade II listed building. The nave was rebuilt in the 14th century, while the tower was added in the

late 15th or early 16th century. The church is no longer in use as a place of worship.

Alton Priors SN8 4LB

- **Knap Hill neolithic earthwork** near Alton Barnes. This is a Neolithic causewayed camp that extends over a four acre site. The ditch has been dated to 3500 BC and pottery from around 2200 BC has been found here. The climb up to the earthwork is quite steep but offers splendid views into the Vale of Pewsey.

  Pewsey Downs SN8 4JX

- **Jones's Mill** is a 29 acre area of fen and woodland to the north east of Pewsey. Designated a biological Site of Special Scientific Interest, its peaty soils are fed by natural springs and it is home to water voles, dragonflies, water shrews and birds including kingfishers, snipe and herons. In spring and summer, the grassland, which is grazed by belted Galloway cattle, has yellow flag irises, lady's smock, water avens, southern marsh and common spotted orchids plus rare plants such as the bog bean, bog pimpernel and flea sedge.

4. FROM THE BRUCE TUNNEL TO NEWBURY

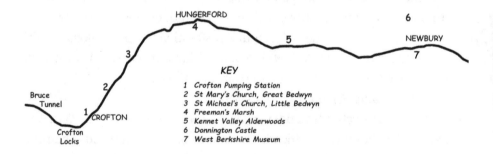

KEY
1 Crofton Pumping Station
2 St Mary's Church, Great Bedwyn
3 St Michael's Church, Little Bedwyn
4 Freeman's Marsh
5 Kennet Valley Alderwoods
6 Donnington Castle
7 West Berkshire Museum

Shortly after the Bruce Tunnel, the locks begin again in earnest, with 20 between here and Hungerford, just over eight miles away, and a further 11 to Newbury. The first set, the Crofton flight of nine, takes the canal down 61 feet.

Some of the locks are quite picturesque. Hungerford Marsh Lock (Lock 73) is unusual in that it has a swing bridge over it and this must be opened before the lock can be used. Although there are more locks in this section than in the last, there are fewer swing bridges.

The countryside between Hungerford and Newbury is particularly beautiful, being lined with high reeds, wildflowers and trees.

In passing: places to visit

- **Crofton Pumping Station** has one of the oldest operational Watt-style beam engines in the world, dating from 1812. However, it is not in use every day (electric pumps now do most of the work) and it is closed for maintenance during the winter months. Its chimney, which has been restored to its original 82 feet, can be seen from some miles away.
  Crofton SN8 3DW
  http://www.croftonbeamengines.org/
- **St. Mary's Church, Great Bedwyn.** Built from a fine grained soft stone together with local flint, this large church has an Early English chancel, early 14th century transepts and late mediaeval aisles, clerestory, and tower. The nave has beautifully moulded and carved capitals and the north transept lies beyond a 14th century wooden screen. Described as one of the finest parish churches in Wiltshire, it houses the tomb of Sir John Seymour whose daughter, Jane, was the third wife of Henry VIII.
  Church Street, Great Bedwyn SN8 3PE
- **St. Michael's Church, Little Bedwyn.** Although some of this grade I listed building may date from the Saxon period, most of it is 12th century and later. Built from flint and rubble, it has a slate roof and a tower that rises to a conical steeple. Most of the windows date from the 15th century. There are beautifully carved column capitals in the nave, each with a unique design, including one with several humorous heads.
  Church Street, Little Bedwyn SN8 3JQ
- **Hungerford** is a pretty market town with a Georgian coaching inn, 18th and 19th century houses and a large number of antiques shops and centres.
- **Freeman's Marsh, Hungerford** runs between the canal and the River Avon and consists of meadows, marsh and reedbed. It is an important site for migratory and breeding birds, and supports many varieties of flora scarce in southern England. Species of birds seen here include the little egret, the little grebe and Cetti's warbler, while hobbys, swifts and yellow wagtails can be seen in the summer and lapwings, redshanks, golden

plovers, redwings and fieldfares are among the winter visitors. It is also a home to water voles.

Just to the north of the canal, between Locks 73 and 74.

- **Kennet Valley Alderwoods.** 140 acres of woodland, designated a Site of Special Scientific Interest, with a great diversity of woodland plants and wildflowers.

Just to the north of the canal, between Locks 78 and 79.

- **Newbury** is a historic market town with many 17th and 18th century listed buildings.

- **Donnington Castle** was built in the 14th century but all except the impressive gatehouse was demolished during the Civil War in the 17th century. During the 15th century the castle belonged to Thomas, the son of the poet Geoffrey Chaucer. Later, Henry VIII and Elizabeth I are both thought to have stayed here. The external walls of the castle have been rebuilt to a height of two feet to show its original layout.

Donnington RG14 2LE

- **West Berkshire Museum, Newbury,** is housed in the 17th century Cloth Hall and the old half-timbered Granary. The collections cover art, science, history and culture and include internationally important finds from the Mesolithic period as well as important collections of Egyptology and objects relating to the English Civil War.

The Wharf, Newbury RG14 5AS

http://www.westberkshireheritage.org/west-berkshire-museum

5. FROM NEWBURY TO READING

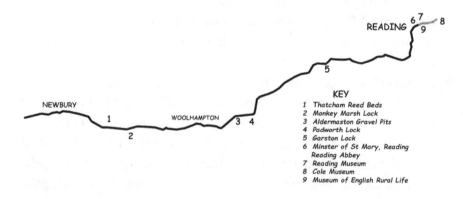

KEY
1 Thatcham Reed Beds
2 Monkey Marsh Lock
3 Aldermaston Gravel Pits
4 Padworth Lock
5 Garston Lock
6 Minster of St Mary, Reading
  Reading Abbey
7 Reading Museum
8 Cole Museum
9 Museum of English Rural Life

Between Newbury and Aldermaston (a stretch of 8½ miles with 10 locks) the canal runs through some beautiful countryside but, soon afterwards, starts to pass more built up areas as it approaches Reading. Between the junction with the River Kennet at Newbury, down to Woolhampton, has been designated a Site of Special Scientific Interest because of the plants and wildlife to be found there.

There is a total of 22 locks on the Newbury to Reading stretch. Just past Lock 95 at Aldermaston is a lift bridge which carries the busy A340 across the canal. Road traffic is stopped by level-crossing type barriers and traffic lights, allowing boats to go through. At Lock 106 (County Lock) the canal enters the centre of Reading and becomes narrow and twisting, with blind bends. In this stretch (known as Brewery Gut because it once flowed through a large brewery) the canal has traffic lights which are controlled by push buttons.

In passing: things to see and do
Places of note:
- **Lock 90 (Monkey Marsh Lock)** at Thatcham is a very rare example of a turf-sided lock and is a scheduled ancient monument. One of only two now remaining on the Kennet & Avon, it was built about 1720. Originally, all the locks were turf sided, the lock chamber being lined below the low water level with vertical planks but, above this level, with turf sloping out at 45 degrees. The main drawback with such locks was that they used vast amounts of water. Although this wasn't a major problem on the River Kennet, most of them were eventually converted into the brick locks we see today.
- **The Kennet & Avon Canal Trust Visitor Centre** at Lock 96 (Padworth Lock) is housed in an old canalman's cottage.
- **Lock 102 (Garston Lock)** is the second turf-sided lock on this canal. It is a particularly good example and has needed less restoration than Monkey Marsh Lock. Beside the lock are two WWII pillboxes - like the lock itself, they are listed buildings.

Places to visit:
- **Thatcham Reed Beds** (between Locks 88 and 89) is a 169 acre Site of Special Scientific Interest where a wide range of birds, dragonflies, damsel

flies and moths can be seen, including some rare species.

Muddy Lane, Lower Way, Thatcham RG19 3FU

http://www.bbowt.org.uk/reserves/thatcham-reedbeds

- **Aldermaston Gravel Pits.** To the south of the canal between Bridge 29 and Aldermaston Wharf, these 57 acres are home to a large number of birds including nine breeding species of warblers, water rails, kingfishers and an important breeding colony of nightingales. The area is managed as a nature reserve by English Nature.

- **The Minster of St. Mary-the-Virgin, Reading.** This is a grade I listed building with origins in the 11th century. It has a Saxon doorway (from the nunnery that was originally on this spot), a 16th century tower and north door, and some fine 19th century stained glass.

  Chain Steet, Reading RG1 2HX

- **Reading Museum** has collections illustrating local history and the local environment. The Huntley and Palmer collection tells the story of the famous 19th-20th century biscuit manufacturers and has many of their colourful biscuit tins on display. The museum also has a full size copy of the Bayeux Tapestry.

  Town Hall, Blagrave Street, Reading RG1 1QH

  http://www.readingmuseum.org.uk/

- **The Cole Museum of Zoology,** housed at Reading University, offers "the whole animal kingdom under one roof" but in a way that will allow a complete tour to be made in about an hour. Highlights of the collection include the skeletons of an Indian elephant, a killer whale, a five metre long python, and a pair of giant spider crabs.

  Ams Building, University of Reading, Whiteknights Campus RG6 6AD

  https://www.reading.ac.uk/colemuseum/

- **Museum of English Rural Life.** This is also housed by the university and illustrates the changing face of farming and the countryside.

  University of Reading, Redlands Road RG1 5EX

  https://www.reading.ac.uk/TheMERL

- **Reading Abbey.** Founded by Henry I in 1121, much of it was destroyed in 1538 during Henry VIII's Dissolution of the Monasteries, but there are fairly extensive ruins. Just north of Bridge 1.

  Abbey Street, Reading RG1 3BA

THE LANCASTER CANAL

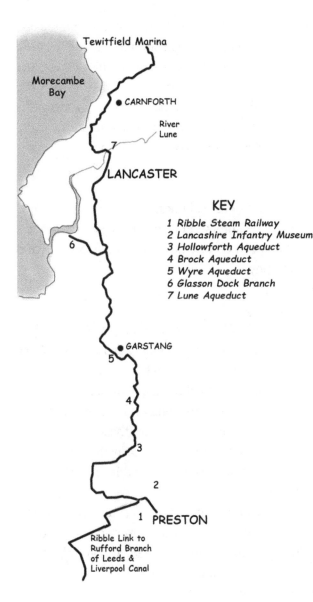

Tewitfield Marina

Morecambe Bay

● CARNFORTH

River Lune

LANCASTER

KEY

1 Ribble Steam Railway
2 Lancashire Infantry Museum
3 Hollowforth Aqueduct
4 Brock Aqueduct
5 Wyre Aqueduct
6 Glasson Dock Branch
7 Lune Aqueduct

● GARSTANG

PRESTON

Ribble Link to
Rufford Branch
of Leeds &
Liverpool Canal

Opened in 1797, this canal originally ran from Preston to Kendal. However, only the southern part is now navigable, and the northern terminus of the canal is at Tewitfield Marina.

This is an ideal canal for those who want a truly leisurely experience. It runs for 42 miles through lovely scenery and has no locks at all. Much of its route is along the foothills of the Pennines but, just north of Lancaster, it is only a few hundred yards from the sea, offering a wonderful view of Morecambe Bay and, beyond it, the mountains of the Lake District.

Shortly after leaving its southern terminus in Preston, the Ribble Link branches off to the south. This waterway, which was opened in 2002, has nine locks and links the Lancaster Canal to the Rufford Branch of the Leeds & Liverpool Canal at Tarleton, via a short trip along the River Ribble itself. All boats have to be guided along the Link and have to be booked in advance - but only experienced boaters should attempt this journey, since the Link is a tidal waterway.

In passing: things to see and do

Places of note:

- **Aqueducts.** There are several short aqueducts along the course of the canal - including the Hollowforth Aqueduct near Woodplumpton (grade II listed), the Brock Aqueduct (built over the River Brock by John Rennie in 1797), and the Wyre Aqueduct over the River Wyre at Garstang (grade II listed). The sandstone Lune Aqueduct, over the River Lune near Skerton, is 220 yards long, grade I listed, and was built in 1797 at a cost of just under £50,000. Recent restoration work, completed in 2012, cost £2.4 million.

Places to visit:

- **The city of Preston** has a wealth of listed buildings.
- **The Harris Museum and Art Gallery, Preston,** housed in a grade I listed building, has collections of fine art, decorative art, costume and textiles, history and photography.
  Market Street, Preston PR1 2PP
  http://www.harrismuseum.org.uk/
- **St. Walburge's Roman Catholic Church** is a grade I listed building. Its 309 foot spire is the third tallest in England, only those of Salisbury and Norwich Cathedrals being higher. The church was built in 1847 by Joseph Aloysius Hansom, who also designed the hansom cab. A large and impressive church, St. Walburge's is 165 feet long and has an intricately carved hammer beam roof. A war memorial set into the south wall has, as its central feature, a mediaeval sculpture of the crucifixion, rescued from a 14th century French abbey that was destroyed during WWI.
  Weston Street, Preston PR2 2QE
- **The Lancashire Infantry Museum.** The collections include artefacts relating to the Queen's Lancashire Regiment and over 100 other units that fought in WWI, including militia, rifle volunteers, territorials, home guard and cadet units as well as 59 batallions.
  Fulwood Barracks, Fulwood, Preston PR2 8AA
  http://www.lancashireinfantrymuseum.org.uk/
- **The Ribble Steam Railway** offers a three mile return trip which goes across the dock swing bridge and along the bank of the River Ribble. There is also a 'hands on' museum with locomotives, carriages and wagons, and an indoor miniature railway.

Chain Caul Road, Preston PR2 2PD

http://www.ribblesteam.org.uk/

- **St. Helen's Church, Churchtown, Garstang,** is a grade I listed building, which dates in part from the 13th century. It has been added to and restored in successive centuries. Interesting features include a 'squint' (a window through which 'undesirables' could watch the service without coming into contact with the worshippers), a grave marker for the village's only victim of the Black Death, and a large rafter supposedly presented to the parish by King Henry VIII.

  Church Street, Churchtown, Garstang PR3 0HW

- **Garstang** is a market town and, since 2000, has been known as the World's First Fairtrade Town. Its Thursday market has been running since 1310. You can download a PDF of a 'heritage trail' walk around the town here: **http://www.garstang.net/heritage_trail.php**

- **Lancaster Castle** was probably built in the 11th century on the site of a Roman fort and has a chequered history, having been used off and on as a prison, most recently between 1955 and 2011. The castle is open every day and offers regular guided tours.

  Castle Park, Lancaster LA1 1YJ

  http://www.lancastercastle.com/

- **Williamson Park, Lancaster.** 54 acres of parkland, woodland walks and play areas with spectacular views of the Fylde coast, Morecambe Bay and the Lake District. Attractions include meerkats and other small animals, and a butterfly house.

  Quernmore Road, Lancaster LA1 1UX

- **Lancaster Priory** is close to Lancaster Castle and is a grade I listed building. The carved oak choir stalls date from 1340 and are the third oldest in England. The pulpit dates from 1619 and the carved font cover from 1631. The church houses a replica of a three foot long runic cross which was found buried in the churchyard in 1807 (the original is now in the British Museum). There is a late 18th century grade II listed sundial in the churchyard.

  Priory Close, Lancaster LA1 1YZ

- **Carnforth Station Heritage Centre.** Carnforth station was the setting for David Lean's iconic 1945 film Brief Encounter. Exhibitions relate to the film itself, life in the 1940s and 'the age of steam'.

  Warton Road, Carnforth LA5 9TR

  http://www.carnforthstation.co.uk/

THE LEEDS & LIVERPOOL CANAL

The Leeds & Liverpool Canal was opened in 1774 and is 127 miles long. It is the longest canal in Britain to have been built as a single waterway (the Grand Union is slightly longer but originated as a number of individual canals which were amalgamated later). Starting in Leeds, where it links with the River Aire and the Aire & Calder Navigation, it crosses the Pennines by means of 91 locks and ends beside the River Mersey in Liverpool,. It has several short branches. Together with five other canals it forms part of the North Pennine Ring and, with eight others, the Outer Pennine Ring. At its highest point, it is 487 feet above sea level.

The Rufford Branch links the canal to the Lancaster Canal, via the Ribble Link (see the section on the Lancaster Canal). The Leigh Branch runs from Wigan to connect with the Bridgewater Canal in Leigh. In Liverpool an extension was completed in 2008 which links the 530 yard long Stanley Dock Branch to the South Docks, via Albert Dock.

Originally the canal was built with locks that were only 60 feet long. Some of these were later extended to 72 feet. A 62 foot boat can get through the whole canal although, between Leeds and Wigan, it may be necessary to fit in diagonally (something that should only be attempted by experienced boaters). The locks between Wigan and Liverpool and those on the Leigh Branch will accommodate 72 foot boats.

The first stretch of the canal, from Leeds to Kirkstall, is 13½ miles long and has 12 locks, of which two (Locks 4 and 5) form a staircase. However, over the next 12 miles there are five sets of staircase locks - Forge Locks (3), Newlay Locks (3), Dobson Locks (2), Field Locks (3) and Dowley Gap Locks (2).

Between Newlay Locks and Dobson Locks there are several bridges. Confusingly, while the locks are numbered from Leeds, the bridges are numbered from Liverpool. Bridge 218 (Moss Swing Bridge) can, according to the website **http://canalplan.eu/**, be very hard to open on hot days. It suggests that you "try pouring quite a few buckets of canal water on to the parts of the bridge that rub to cool the metal down. If this doesn't help call: Yorkshire Water, Tel. 0844-9022991."

At Bingley there are two flights of staircase locks, the first having three locks and the second (which is the highest and steepest staircase in Britain)

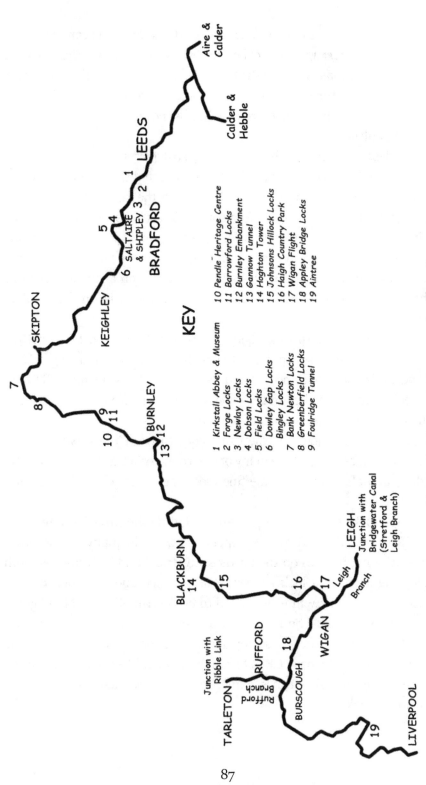

KEY

1 Kirkstall Abbey & Museum
2 Forge Locks
3 Newlay Locks
4 Dobson Locks
5 Field Locks
6 Dowley Gap Locks
  Bingley Locks
7 Bank Newton Locks
8 Greenberfield Locks
9 Foulridge Tunnel
10 Pendle Heritage Centre
11 Barrowford Locks
12 Burnley Embankment
13 Gannow Tunnel
14 Haghton Tower
15 Johnsons Hillock Locks
16 Haigh Country Park
17 Wigan Flight
18 Appley Bridge Locks
19 Aintree

Aire & Calder

Calder & Hebble

LEEDS

BRADFORD

SALTAIRE & SHIPLEY

KEIGHLEY

SKIPTON

BURNLEY

BLACKBURN

LEIGH

Junction with Bridgewater Canal (Stretford & Leigh Branch)

Leigh Branch

WIGAN

BURSCOUGH

RUFFORD

Rufford Branch

TARLETON

Junction with Ribble Link

LIVERPOOL

The Leeds & Liverpool Canal

87

having five. Both flights have lock keepers in attendance. You can then enjoy 17½ miles of uninterrupted travel before you reach the next series of twelve locks, of which the last six form the Bank Newton Flight. Another four miles further on and the three Greenberfield Locks are reached which take you to the summit and a six mile flat stretch which is, however, interrupted by the mile-long Foulridge Tunnel.

The descent begins with the seven Barrowford Locks, after which a long flat stretch of just over 23 miles takes the canal through Burnley and on (via the 558 yard long Gannow Tunnel) to the six Blackburn Locks. After eight miles come the seven Johnsons Hillock Locks and the canal then continues in a southerly direction for another nine miles before reaching the 21 locks that make up the Wigan Flight. Very shortly after this, the Leigh Branch departs southwards and there are then a further six locks in the next six miles before you reach the last three locks on the canal, at Appley Bridge.

In its final 28 or so miles between Appley Bridge and Liverpool the canal crosses 16 short aqueducts but goes through no locks. Swing bridges 6, 9 and 16 (Netherton, Hancocks and Bells Lane) are manned by CRT staff but opening times may be limited - check with your hire company if you're intending to explore this section of the canal.

During its long journey, the canal goes through the urban areas of Burnley and Blackburn, where many of the old Victorian cotton mills are still standing, and also through some fine moorland scenery and the beautiful Yorkshire dales.

All the locks from Leeds up to and including the three Newlay Locks need CRT and handcuff keys to open them, as do many of the other locks and swing bridges on the Leeds & Liverpool and its branches. Both Bingley flights have a lock keeper in attendance and are open only at specific times (in the winter you need to book a time if you intend going through these locks). The Bingley lock keeper also controls Bridge 200 (immediately above the 5-rise top lock). The locks from Leeds to the Newlay Flight usually have CRT staff on hand and, like the Bingley Locks, have restricted opening times while, in winter, passage through them needs to be booked.

Branches

The Rufford Branch is 7 ¼ miles long and has eight locks. It leaves the main line at Burscough and runs to Tarleton where it meets the Ribble Link, travelling through some pretty countryside but, in many places, having high vegetation on either side. Boaters should be aware that the winding hole at Tarleton is tight, so turning even a 60 foot boat needs care. If you are uncertain of your winding skills or have a longer boat, you should wind at Rufford, shortly after Lock 7 (Rufford Lock). Many of the swing bridges and locks on this branch need a CRT key to open them.

The 7½ mile long Leigh Branch leaves the main line at Wigan, passes through two locks, and meets the Stretford & Leigh Branch of the Bridgewater Canal, not surprisingly, in Leigh.

The Springs Branch in Skipton is only half a mile long and has no locks.

In passing: things to see and do

Places of note on the main line

- **Burnley embankment.** Known locally as 'The Straight Mile', the embankment was built between 1796 and 1801 to carry the canal across the Calder Valley, avoiding the need for locks. Sixty feet high, it gives views right across the town. The canal takes a sharp turn to enter its southern end.
- **Aintree.** The canal passes close to the racecourse where the Grand National is run. The fence nearest the canal, where horses have to make a sharp left hand turn, is known as Canal Turn.

Places to visit on the main line
(For more places in Leeds, see the listings in the section on the Aire & Calder Navigations.)
- **Leeds Cathedral** is one of the finest Roman Catholic cathedrals in England and is a grade II* listed building. Completed in 1904, it was restored in 2006. The altarpiece in the lady chapel was designed by Augustus Pugin and was previously part of the high altar of the old cathedral which this building replaced.
Great George Street, Leeds LS2 8BE
http://www.dioceseofleeds.org.uk/cathedral/

- **Kirkgate Market, Leeds,** is one of the largest indoor markets in Europe and for two years running has been voted Britain's Favourite Market at the 'Great British Market Awards' .
Vicar Lane, Leeds City Centre LS2 7HY
- **The Industrial Museum at Armley Mills.** Housed in a grade II* listed building that was once the world's largest woollen mill, the museum has exhibitions on textiles, tailoring, industry and printing, with exhibits including a working waterwheel, factory machinery, and restored Victorian workers' cottages together with a 1920s cinema where you can watch a black and white film. Close to Bridge 225 (Mill Bridge).
Canal Road, Armley, Leeds LS12 2QF
- **Kirkstall Abbey.** Although roofless, this ruined Cistercian monastery is one of the most complete mediaeval monastic sites in Britain. Built in the mid 12th century, the abbey is a grade I listed building and scheduled ancient monument. Interactive exhibits illustrate the history of the abbey and the lives of the monks.
Abbey Road, Leeds LS5 3EH
- **Abbey House Museum, Kirkstall,** is housed in the gatehouse of Kirkstall Abbey. The ground floor is set out as an area of Victorian streets, while the upstairs galleries have displays relating to childhood, the history of Kirkstall Abbey, and the social history of Leeds,
Abbey Road, Leeds LS5 3EH
- **Saltaire.** Built along the River Aire in the mid 19th century by Sir Titus Salt, Saltaire consists of textile mills and the town where the mill workers lived. It is now a World Heritage Site.
- **Salt Mills, Saltaire,** opened as a textile mill in 1853. It was closed in 1986 and, soon afterwards, was turned into a multi-purpose space with offices, restaurants, shops and exhibitions. The 1853 Gallery has the world's largest permanent collection of work by Bradford-born artist, David Hockney. There is also a permanent exhibition on the history of Saltaire.
Victoria Road, Shipley, Saltaire BD18 3LA
http://www.saltsmill.org.uk/
- **Shipley Glen Tramway.** Opened in 1895, this is the oldest funicular tramway in the UK. Its original purpose was to give easier access to the massive fairground which had opened in 1870 at Bracken Hall Green.

Prod Lane, Baildon, Shipley BD17 5BN

http://www.shipleyglentramway.co.uk/index.html

- **East Riddlesden Hall** is owned by the National Trust and consists of a grade I listed manor house, built in 1642, and a mediaeval tithe barn. On display is some fine furniture, English pewter and needlework, all dating from the 17th to 19th centuries, as well as impressive plasterwork ceilings. The tithe barn, which is said to be one of the best in northern England, houses a collection of wheeled vehicles.

Bradford Road, Riddlesden, Keighley, BD20 5EL

- **Cliffe Castle Museum, Keighley.** Housed in a Victorian mansion, with extensive gardens and an aviary, the museum displays Victorian rooms and furniture, paintings, and decorative art. There are galleries dealing with natural history, archaeology and social history, and an important display of stained glass by Morris and Co. A section on geology has fossils ranging from ammonites and ichthyosaurs of the Jurassic period to an important holotype of Pholiderpeton scutigerum, an amphibian from the Carboniferous period.

Spring Gardens Lane, Keighley BD20 6LH

- **Skipton Castle.** Built in 1090 as a wooden motte and bailey and strengthened with stone in the 12th century, this is one of most complete and best preserved English mediaeval castles. The banqueting hall, kitchen, bedchamber and privy, dungeons and watch tower are open to the public.

Skipton BD23 1AW

http://www.skiptoncastle.co.uk/

- **Craven Museum and Gallery** is housed in Skipton Town Hall. The museum tells the story of the southern part of the Yorkshire Dales known as Craven and has displays of social history, archaeology, costume and art. It also has one of only four Shakespeare First Folios to be on permanent display.

Town Hall, High Street, Skipton BD23 1AH

http://www.cravenmuseum.org/

- **Holy Trinity Church, Skipton.** Built about 1300, the church was extended in the late 15th century and is a grade I listed building. The tower and some of the windows were damaged during the Civil War, but were restored soon afterwards.

Mill Bridge, Skipton BD23 1NJ

- **Pendle Heritage Centre, Burnley.** The museum focuses on local history including the 17th century Pendle witches, George Fox and the Quaker movement (Society of Friends) and the Bannister family - ancestors of Roger Bannister, first man to run a mile in under four minutes.
  Colne Road, Barrowford, Burnley BB9 6JQ
  http://www.pendleheritage.co.uk/
- **Blackburn Museum & Art Gallery.** Housed in a grade II listed building, the museum has collections of paintings, Japanese prints, mediaeval manuscripts, natural history, ancient Egyptian artefacts, coins and much else. Opened in 1874, it was one of the first purpose-built free museums outside London.
  Museum Street, Blackburn BB1 7AJ
  http://blackburnmuseum.org.uk/
- **Hoghton Tower** is a 16th century fortified hilltop manor house with beautiful gardens. Royal guests have included James I, William III and George V. There are state rooms, a banqueting hall, minstrels' gallery and dungeons, as well as a collection of 27 beautifully furnished dolls' houses dating from the 19th and 20th centuries.
  Hoghton PR5 0SH
  http://www.hoghtontower.co.uk/
- **Haigh Country Park** near Wigan has 350 acres of wood and parkland with nature trails, a miniature railway, an 18 hole golf course that is both scenic and challenging - and an 18 hole crazy golf course.
  Copperas Lane, Haigh WN2 1PE
- **The Museum of Wigan Life** holds collections of art, archaeology, natural history, coins and artefacts relating to local life and industry.
  Library Street, Wigan WN1 1NU
- **Trencherfield Mill,** built in 1907, houses the world's largest original working steam engine. It is open only on Sundays, with tours starting at 11am and 1pm.
  Wigan Pier Quarter, Heritage Way, Wigan WN3 4EF

A place to visit on the Rufford Branch:
- **Rufford Old Hall,** a fine timber-framed manor house dating from about 1530, is now owned by the National Trust. It has an interesting collection of 16th century arms & armour, 17th century furniture, and paintings.
  200 Liverpool Road, Rufford L40 1SG

THE LLANGOLLEN CANAL

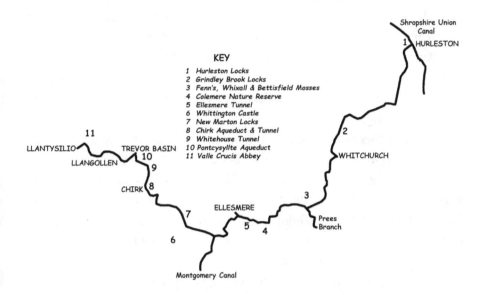

KEY

1 Hurleston Locks
2 Grindley Brook Locks
3 Fenn's, Whixall & Bettisfield Mosses
4 Colemere Nature Reserve
5 Ellesmere Tunnel
6 Whittington Castle
7 New Marton Locks
8 Chirk Aqueduct & Tunnel
9 Whitehouse Tunnel
10 Pontcysyllte Aqueduct
11 Valle Crucis Abbey

The Llangollen Canal runs from Hurleston in Cheshire to Llantysilio in north Wales, by way of Ellesmere in Shropshire. It is a narrow canal (in some places, very narrow), having been built as a navigable feeder branch for the Ellesmere Canal (which was never completed) rather than as a canal in its own right. It is 46 miles long, has 21 locks and is said to be the most popular canal in Britain.

The canal connects with the Shropshire Union Canal at Hurleston and with the navigable upper end of the Montgomery Canal at Lower Frankton. It also has four short arms: the quarter mile long Whitchurch Arm, the Prees Branch (of which a mile and a half has been restored), the quarter mile long Ellesmere Arm, and the Trevor Basin which is just an eighth of a mile long. None of them has any locks, but the Prees Branch has two lift bridges.

Immediately after Hurleston junction you come to four locks and there are a further nine in the next 12 miles. Also in this stretch is Wrenbury Lift Bridge which needs a CRT key and involves closing barriers and stopping traffic on a road that can be busy.

The canal then reaches the six Grindley Brook Locks, the last three of which form a staircase. During the summer months, a lock keeper is in attendance. After a further 6½ lock-free miles, the Prees Branch departs to the south. The 10 miles between here and the junction with the Montgomery Canal (at Frankton Junction) is interrupted only by the 87 yard long Ellesmere Tunnel. Three miles further on, the canal reaches the two New Marton Locks which are said to be among the busiest locks in Britain.

Another 2¾ miles on, and you have reached the eleven mile long final section. In places it's very narrow, making it impossible for boats to pass each other, so someone needs to go ahead with a mobile 'phone and ring back when the passage is clear.

In 2009 this last section was declared a World Heritage Site, and it is this section that draws the crowds - but if you suffer from claustrophobia or fear of heights you may wish to avoid it! First comes the Chirk Aqueduct which, like that at Pontcysyllte further along the canal, was built by Thomas Telford and William Jessop and was one of the first to use a cast iron trough to carry the canal. Chirk's trough rests on conventional masonry arches and is hidden inside the masonry itself. Built in 1801, it's 68 feet high, just under 240 yards long and runs across the Ceiriog Valley, crossing the border from England to Wales. Next to it is a railway viaduct, built in the 1840s, which, being 30 feet higher than the aqueduct, has the effect of making the latter seem less high than it actually is.

Almost immediately after the aqueduct comes the 460 yard Chirk Tunnel and, a little further on, the 165 yard Whitehouse Tunnel, which were the first in Britain to include towpaths. And then it's just a mile and a half to the Pontcysyllte Aqueduct, the tallest navigable aqueduct in Britain, 126 feet high and 335 yards long. It feels much less substantial than the Chirk Aqueduct. There is no accompanying viaduct dwarfing it, and the trough is exposed and rests on slender masonry towers. The towpath (for intrepid walkers) has solid railings along the side - but on the other side there is nothing. If you're not worried by heights, the views are spectacular. If you are worried by heights, it's probably best to sit inside the boat and read a book while another member of the crew steers the boat across.

Once across the aqueduct, five miles of lock-free canal brings you to the pretty town of Llangollen, which is as far as you can go. Powered boats are not allowed on the 1½ miles of canal leading to Llantysilio and the Horseshoe Falls, which are only accessible by taking a trip on a horse-drawn narrowboat or by walking along the towpath.

In passing: places to visit

- **Whitchurch** has a number of half timbered buildings. The Old Eagles pub in Watergate Street is the oldest building, probably dating from the 14th century. However, it only became a pub about 150 years ago.

- **St. Alkmund's Church, Whitchurch.** Built in 1713, this grade I listed building is the largest Georgian church in the county outside Shrewsbury. Church Street, Whitchurch SY13 1LB

- **Greenfields Nature Reserve.** Grassland and woodland where you may see water voles, kingfishers, woodpeckers, nuthatches and butterflies. A leaflet can be downloaded here:
  http://www.malcolm.monie.care4free.net/GF%20LEAFLET%20 FOR%20WEB.pdf
  Meadowcroft, Whitchurch SY13 1BD

- **Whitchurch Heritage Centre** has exhibits on Roman and mediaeval history, clocks (particularly those made by the local firm of Joyce), and the composer Edward German (who was born locally). Many of the exhibits are 'hands-on' and are geared towards children.
  12 St. Mary's Street, Whitchurch SY13 1QY
  http://www.whitchurch-heritage.co.uk/

- **Fenn's, Whixall & Bettisfield Mosses National Nature Reserve.** Covering 2340 acres, this is a rare survivor since most similar areas have been drained, forested or become commercial peat bogs. This area was used commercially until 1990, since when restoration of the mosses has been carried out. It provides a habitat for 166 species of birds (including kingfishers, curlew, teal, shovellers and various raptors), 29 species of damselflies and dragonflies, 32 species of butterfly (including the brimstone, the green hairstreak and the large heath) as well as watervoles, and very rare picture-winged bog craneflies. There are numerous bog-loving plants including 18 species of bog moss (some of which are very rare), the insect-eating round-leaved sundew, bog asphodel, bog rosemary, lesser bladderwort, white-beaked sedge, bog myrtle, water figwort, flag iris, alder buckthorn, grey sallow and crack willow. A leaflet and map can be downloaded here:
  http://publications.naturalengland.org.uk/file/65041

- **Colemere Nature Reserve.** Three miles south east of Ellesmere, this Site of Special Scientific Interest consists of mature woodland and hay meadows surrounding a large expanse of water where you can see a wide variety of birds including snipe, curlew, goldeneye, and pochard. In the spring and summer, flowers such as southern marsh orchids, meadow cranesbill and lady's smock grow in the meadows and the brown hawker dragonfly and common blue damselfly can be seen. It is also the only place in England where the Least Water Lily is found.

off Ellesmere Road, near the village of Colemere SY12 0Q

- **St. Mary's Church, Ellesmere.** Built by the Knights of St. John, this grade I listed church dates in part to the 13th century. The 15th century chantry chapel has a carved roof said to be one of the finest in Shropshire. In the 19th century, the nave was redesigned by George Gilbert Scott. The chancel is paved with Minton tiles and the sanctuary with Belgian marble. In the churchyard there is a sundial dated 1726 which is grade II listed.

Church Hill, Ellesmere SY12 0HB

- **Whittington Castle** consists of extensive ruins set in 12 acres of grounds. Still standing are the inner bailey, great hall, keep, well and dovecote, and two imposing gatehouse towers, into one of which a 17th century cottage is built.

Castle Street, Whittington SY11 4DF

http://www.whittingtoncastle.co.uk/

- **Chirk Castle.** Dating from 1310, and lived in by the same family since 1595, Chirk Castle is now managed by the National Trust. It houses an eclectic collection of beautiful objects including Chippendale furniture and fine tapestries in rooms that include the 17th century long gallery, 18th century saloon and 1920s style Bow Room. There are 5½ acres of beautiful gardens, including an 18th century ha-ha, plus 480 acres of parkland with wild ponies and a very well preserved section of Offa's Dyke. It has been designated a Site of Special Scientific Interest and is an important habitat for rare bats, fungi and wild flowers.

Chirk LL14 5AF

https://www.nationaltrust.org.uk/chirk-castle

- **Castell Dinas Bran (Crow Castle).** Perched on top of a hill overlooking Llangollen, little is left of the castle but it offers spectacular views of Llangollen and the Dee Valley which make the steep climb worthwhile. Legend has it that the Holy Grail may be buried here. In the 13th century it was the home of Madoc ap Gruffydd Maelor, who founded Valle Crucis Abbey.

Llangollen LL20 8DY

http://www.castlewales.com/dinas.html

- **Llangollen railway** is the only standard gauge heritage railway in North Wales. It offers a 10 mile trip along the Dee Valley (a Site of Special Scientific Interest) to the town of Corwen, passing through some beautiful scenery.
The Station, Abbey Road, Llangollen LL20 8SN
http://www.llangollen-railway.co.uk/

- **Plas Newydd.** Between 1780 and 1829 this was the home of Lady Eleanor Butler and Miss Sarah Ponsonby who became known as 'the Ladies of Llangollen'. It is now one of Wales' most famous tourist attractions. It contains some of their possessions and retains the stained glass and elaborate oak carving that they installed as part of their conversion of their original little cottage into an extraordinary Gothic-style house. The gardens offer a splendid view of Castell Dinas Bran.
Hill Street, Llangollen LL20 8AW

- **St. Collen's Church, Llangollen,** was built in 1450 and extensively renovated in the Victorian era. Its splendid carved oak ceiling is thought to date from the 15th century.
Regent Street, Llangollen LL20 8HL

- **Valle Crucis Abbey** dates from the 13th century and is 2 miles from Llangollen. Much of it was destroyed by Henry VIII but many original features remain, including the west front with its elaborately carved doorway, the rose window, the east end of the abbey, the monks' original fishpond, and the chapter house with its rib-vaulted roof.
Llantysilio, Llangollen LL20 8DD
http://cadw.gov.wales/daysout/vallecrucisabbey/?lang=en

THE MACCLESFIELD CANAL

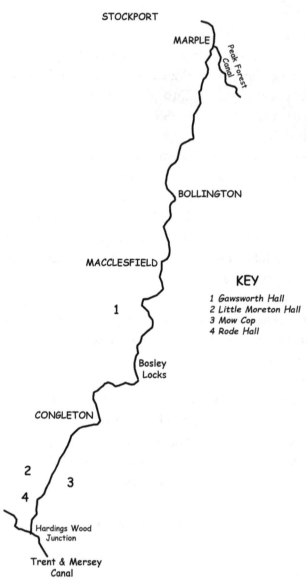

STOCKPORT

MARPLE

Peak Forest Canal

BOLLINGTON

MACCLESFIELD

KEY

1 Gawsworth Hall
2 Little Moreton Hall
3 Mow Cop
4 Rode Hall

1

Bosley Locks

CONGLETON

2

3

4

Hardings Wood Junction

Trent & Mersey Canal

This canal is 26 miles long and is one of the six that make up the Cheshire Ring, the others being the Trent & Mersey, Bridgewater, Rochdale, Ashton and Peak Forest. It starts from the junction with the Peak Forest Canal at Marple and finishes at Hardings Wood Junction, near Kidsgrove, where it joins the Hall Green Branch of the Trent & Mersey. Over its course it encounters 13 locks (all except one occurring in a stretch of about a mile at Bosley), eight short aqueducts, and two swing bridges. The 13th lock is just above the junction with the Trent & Mersey.

All the locks, and nearly half of the 95 bridges that cross the canal are grade II listed. So, too, are five of the aqueducts (Dane, Biddulph Valley, Canal Road, Red Bull and Pool Lock) all of which are in the section between the Bosley Locks and Hardings Wood Junction. Pool Lock Aqueduct is at the junction itself, taking the Macclesfield over the Trent & Mersey before the two canals actually meet. There are a number of roving bridges which, locally, are known as snake bridges.

The locks are unusual for a narrow canal, in that both ends have paired mitre gates, rather than the top gate being single. Bridges 47 and 49 need a CRT key, while Bridge 22 needs a windlass and handcuff key.

Mostly, the canal travels through pleasant rural surroundings, and much of its course runs parallel to the Peak District National Park. In 2015 it was the first canal in the country to be awarded a Green Flag in the Keep Britain Tidy Award Scheme.

In passing: places to visit

- **Bollington Discovery Centre.** Located in an old cotton mill by the side of the canal, this centre tells how cotton changed Bollington and the surrounding area from an agricultural backwater to an industrial town.
  Clarence Mill, Clarence Road, Bollington, SK10 5JZ
- **The Silk Museum, Macclesfield,** has collections relating both to the manufacture of silk and to the people who worked in the silk industry.
  Park Lane, Macclesfield, SK11 6TJ
  https://macclesfieldmuseums.co.uk/venues/the-silk-museum
- **West Park Museum, Macclesfield,** houses a collection of Egyptian artefacts amassed by Victorian explorer Marianne Brocklehurst. Other exhibits relate to local history and there is a collection of the works of the internationally renowned wildlife artist Charles Tunnicliffe who was born nearby.
  Prestbury Road, Macclesfield SK10 3BJ
  http://www.silkmacclesfield.org.uk/museums/west-park-museum
- **Gawsworth Hall** is a black and white manor house built in 1480, with sculpture, furniture, paintings and stained glass on display. The grounds contain a rookery, tilting ground and Elizabethan pleasure garden. The chapel predates the Hall itself, although it was extensively remodelled at the start of the 18th century. Still in use, it has stained glass and a beautiful panelled roof. The house was the home of Mary Fitton, said to be the Dark Lady of Shakespeare's sonnets.
  Church Lane, Gawsworth SK11 9RN
  http://www.gawsworthhall.com/
- **Little Moreton Hall** is a black and white timber framed building surrounded by a moat, about half a mile from the canal. The house was built in the early 16th century and added to in the following 100 years. Owned by the National

Trust, it has been described as the finest half-timbered manor house in England. Inside the house you can see painted leather panelling, ornately carved fireplaces, a collection of pewter, and a long gallery with mullioned windows, plaster friezes and elaborately carved woodwork. There is a herb garden and a 17th century knot garden. A leaflet can be downloaded here: **https://www.nationaltrust.org.uk/little-moreton-hall/documents/ little-moreton-hall-little-pocket-guide-2016-pdf.pdf** Congleton Road, Congleton CW12 4SD

- **Rode Hall** was built in 1708 and added to in the succeeding 90 years. It houses an important collection of English pottery and porcelain, collected from the mid 18th century onwards by the Wilbraham family who owned the Hall. There are also paintings and pieces of furniture by Gillow. Church Lane, Scholar Green ST7 3QP http://rodehall.co.uk/

- **Mow Cop Castle** is a folly built in 1754 as a summer house by the local Lord of the Manor, who lived at Rode Hall three miles away. It has spectacular views of the Staffordshire moors and the Cheshire Plain. It fell into disrepair at the end of the 19th century and was taken on by the National Trust in 1937. It played an important role in the birth of the Primitive Methodist movement when a large 14 hour long meeting was held there in 1810. Mow Cop ST7 3PA

THE MONMOUTHSHIRE & BRECON CANAL

This canal runs for 35 miles from the Brecon Basin to the Five Locks Basin in Cwmbran. Originally it consisted of two canals - the Monmouthshire Canal (running from Pontymoile to Newport) whose purpose was to carry coal down to the docks, and the Brecknock & Abergavenny Canal (running from Brecon to Pontymoile). Almost all its route is through the Brecon Beacons National Park and much of it runs alongside the tree lined River Usk. It is a very peaceful and exceptionally beautiful canal, with only six locks and it can be cruised very easily in a week. Swans, kingfishers, herons and buzzards, red kites and dragonflies. are common along its length. There are no links with other waterways.

The first lock (Brynich Lock) is just over two miles from the start of the canal. Another 5¾ miles brings you to the quarter mile long Ashford Tunnel. A mile and a half later you come to the five Llangynidr locks which are spread over about half a mile. And then it's 24 miles of lock-free cruising to the end of the canal. There are several lift bridges along the course of the canal - the bridge near Talybont is electrically powered and opening times are restricted to allow children to cross safely on their way to and from school.

In passing: things to see and do

Places of note:

- **Ashford Tunnel.** You can still see notches in the walls that were used by the boatmen to pole their boats through.
- **Goytre Wharf.** Disused limekilns are visible in several places along the canal but some of the best preserved are at Goytre Wharf. Noticeboards around the site explain how they worked. Lime was important both as a fertiliser and a building material. In the late 19th century cheaper ways of producing lime were discovered and the kilns fell into disrepair. The toll collector's office used to be housed in the cottage next to the kilns and the aqueduct.
  http://www.goytrewharf.com/

Places to visit:

- **Brecon Cathedral.** The cathedral and the surrounding buildings were formerly part of a Benedictine priory. In 1923, its status was elevated from parish church to cathedral and the Havard Chapel was turned into a memorial to the South Wales Borderers (the 24th Regiment of Foot) and the Monmouthshire Regiment. The colours of the 1st Battalion the 24th Regiment of Foot which served in the 1879 Zulu War are on display. The cathedral also has the largest Norman font in Wales. It is thought to date from the mid 12th century (although it could be earlier) and is decorated with grotesque carvings.
  Cathedral Close, Brecon LD3 9DP
- **Brecon Heritage Centre.** This is housed in a 17th century tithe barn in the cathedral close. It tells the story of Brecon Priory from when it was built in 1093 to the present day.
  Cathedral Close, Brecon LD3 9DP
- **The Regimental Museum** of The Royal Welsh holds one of the finest collections of military artefacts in Britain. There are displays relating to the Zulu wars and both World Wars. Exhibits, which span the last 300 years, include over 3000 medals as well as paintings, drums, buttons, badges, uniforms and weapons.

The Barracks, Watton, Brecon LD3 7EB

http://www.royalwelsh.org.uk/regimental-museum-of-the-royal- welsh. shtml

- **Brecknock Museum.** Housed in the old Shire Hall, a grade II* listed building, this has been described as one of the finest small museums in Wales. Collections include local archaeological and geological material, social history and natural history collections and art. Among the exhibits are a rare mediaeval log boat, prehistoric tools, Roman metalwork, traditional Welsh furniture and paintings by Augustus John, John Piper, Eric Ravilious and Graham Sutherland.

  Captains Walk, Brecon LD3 7DS

  http://www.powys.gov.uk/en/museums/visit-your-local-museum/ brecknock-museum-art-gallery/

- **Tretower Court** is a mediaeval fortified manor house and dates in part from the early 14th century. In the 19th century it became a working farm but, by the early 20th, the building was in a serious state of disrepair. It was saved for the nation in the 1930s and has been restored, with a suite of rooms now furnished as they might have been in the late 15th century.

  Crickhowell NP8 1RD

- **St. Catwg's Church, Llangattock.** The oldest part of the building is the tower, which dates from the 12th century. Although the church has seen considerable restoration in the last two centuries, much of the original remains. The arcade of arches running down the centre of the church was erected in the 14th century and the main porch dates from the Tudor period. On display are the stocks and whipping post that, in the 18th century, stood at the foot of the tower. A guidebook to the church can be downloaded here:

  http://www.llangattockchurch.org/wp-content/uploads/2012/01/ Guidebook.pdf

  Llangattock NP8 1PH

- **Abergavenny Castle.** First built in 1087, the castle was destroyed in 1233 and rebuilt. The two towers were probably built at the very end of the 13th century and the gatehouse added early in the 15th. Much of it was destroyed in the mid 17th century during the civil war. It is one of the best examples of a motte and bailey castle in Britain.

  Castle Street, Abergavenny NP7 5EE

- **Abergavenny Museum** was formerly a hunting lodge, built in 1818, in the grounds of Abergavenny Castle. It holds collections of local significance with an emphasis on rural life, agriculture and its associated industries and domestic and working life. Among the permanent displays are the contents of a 19th century Welsh kitchen, an early 20th century saddler's shop and a mid 20th century grocery shop. There are also important collections of archaeological material and of costume, and a programme of activities for children.
Castle Street, Abergavenny NP7 5EE
http://www.abergavennymuseum.co.uk/index.php?lang=EN
- **St. Mary's Priory Church, Abergavenny,** was founded in 1087 as a Benedictine Priory but is perhaps more interesting for its contents than for the building itself. A larger than life figure, carved from a single piece of oak, probably in the 15th century, and originally highly coloured, once formed the base of a sculpture depicting the lineage of Jesus. It is known as a Jesse figure. Such figures are not uncommon in stone and stained glass but this is the only wooden one in the UK - and possibly in the world. Lovers of needlework should see the beautiful wall hangings in the baptistry, made by hand by a member of the congregation using antique fabrics, and, in the adjacent tithe barn, the 24 foot long Abergavenny Tapestry, made by sixty local volunteers to celebrate the new millenium.
Monk Street, Abergavenny NP7 5ND
- **Pontypool Museum.** Housed in a Georgian stable block, the museum holds over 15,000 items in its collections, ranging from prehistoric objects to mediaeval and industrial revolution artefacts as well as fine and decorative art, including examples of Pontypool Japanware.
Park Buildings, Park Road, Pontypool NP4 6JH
http://pontypoolmuseum.org.uk/

THE MONTGOMERY CANAL

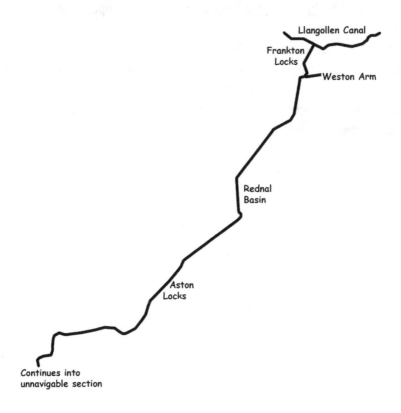

Completed in 1821, the Montgomery Canal was originally 33 miles long, running from its junction with the Llangollen Canal at Frankton down to Newtown. However, today only the upper seven miles are navigable, from Frankton Junction to Gronwyn Wharf. Most of the canal has been designated a Site of Special Scientific Interest, as a result of which only 1250 boats a year are allowed access and there are stricter speed restrictions than on other canals.

Almost immediately after the Frankton Junction, the canal runs through the four Frankton Locks. A lock keeper is in attendance and passage through the locks (which has to be booked in advance) is limited to 12 boats a day. After a quarter of a mile comes the junction with the old Weston Arm, most of which has been infilled and has been converted into a nature reserve. What remains of the Weston Arm is used for mooring.

Another lock follows the junction and then there is a run of 3¾ miles before the three Aston Locks are reached. After this, there is another 2¾ miles of lock-free cruising before the end of the canal. In this final section, Crofts Mill Lift Bridge (Bridge 81) needs a windlass to operate it.

In passing: things to see and do
The main attraction of the Montgomery Canal is its natural beauty. There are nature reserves at various points along the canal, including Rednal Basin, most of the Weston Branch, and a reserve next to the Aston Locks. The canal is home to otters and water voles.

THE OXFORD CANAL

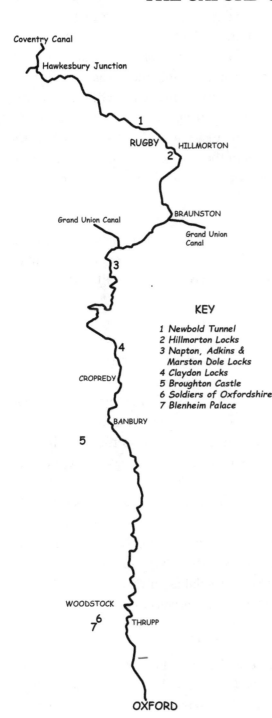

Coventry Canal

Hawkesbury Junction

1

RUGBY   HILLMORTON

2

Grand Union Canal   BRAUNSTON

Grand Union
Canal

3

KEY

1 *Newbold Tunnel*
2 *Hillmorton Locks*
3 *Napton, Adkins &*
  Marston Dole Locks
4 *Claydon Locks*
5 *Broughton Castle*
6 *Soldiers of Oxfordshire*
7 *Blenheim Palace*

4

CROPREDY

BANBURY

5

WOODSTOCK

7 6   THRUPP

OXFORD

This 77 mile long canal runs from Hawkesbury Junction (where it meets the Coventry Canal just north of the city) to Oxford where it connects with the River Thames. With the Grand Union, Birmingham & Fazeley and Coventry Canals, it forms the Warwickshire Ring, linking to the Grand Union at Braunston and sharing its course for five miles to Napton-on-the-Hill, where the two canals separate again.

It has a total of 43 locks. The first of these is very close to the junction with the Coventry Canal but there is then a 15½ mile stretch, interrupted only by the 270 yard long Newbold Tunnel, before the three Hillmorton Locks are reached. A further 14 miles takes you to Napton, and through nine locks (six Napton Locks, Adkins Lock, and the two Marston Doles Locks) in the space of two miles. A final 11 mile stretch of uninterrupted canal brings you to the five Claydon Locks. This part of the canal is very winding and, in fact, Marston Doles and Claydon Locks are only five miles apart as the crow flies). There are a further 25 locks to the end of the canal, but the stretches between them are much shorter from now on.

In the last flat stretch, before Claydon Locks are reached, there is a ¾ mile straight section known as Fenny Compton Tunnel (roughly between Bridges 137 and 139). When the canal was first built, there was a tunnel here but it was only wide enough for one boat to go through at a time and, in the late 19th century, it was opened up into a cutting, to ease the congestion.

A little under seven miles from Claydon Locks, the canal reaches Banbury where there are moorings in the middle of the town, next to the shopping centre. A further 27 miles on, the canal reaches Oxford and its junction with the River Thames.

There are a number of lift bridges over the course of the canal, expecially south of Banbury. Some of these are usually left open. Always leave a bridge the way you found it (unless, of course, a boat just in front of you has deliberately left one open for you to come through after it).

In passing: things to see and do
Places of note:
- **Thrupp** is a pretty canalside village with thatched cottages
- **Hilmorton locks.** In the 1830s reconstruction of parts of the canal to shorten it by 11 miles resulted in increased traffic and a permanent bottleneck at Hillmorton. The paired locks were built in 1840 to ease this, connections being put in between the pairs so they could act as side ponds for each other, allowing a much more economical use of water.
- **Cropredy toll office,** which dates to about 1778, can be seen next to the canal. An oak beam would be lowered until the tonnage had been established and the tolls had been paid. Stables behind the Red Lion public house offered overnight shelter to the narrow boat horses.
- **Wildlife.** There is a wide variety of wildlife on this canal. In Oxford, special measures have been put in place to protect a colony of water voles.

Places to visit:
- **Rugby Art Gallery and Museum.** The collections include 20th century British art (with works by L. S. Lowry, Stanley Spencer and Graham Sutherland), artefacts from the Romano-British town of Tripontium

(situated five miles from the centre of modern Rugby) and 25,000 glass slides from a local, mid 20th century photography studio.

Little Elborow Street. Rugby CV21 3BZ

http://www.ragm.co.uk

- **World Rugby Hall of Fame.** A must for anyone interested in rugby football!

  Little Elborow Street, Rugby, CV21 3BZ

  http://www.therugbytown.co.uk/therugbytown/homepage/2/world_rugby_hall_of_fame

- **The Webb Ellis Rugby Football Museum.** Housed in the former workshop of William Gilbert (who made the first ever rugby balls) the museum holds a unique collection of rugby artefacts and memorabilia, illustrating four themes - the history of the game, its development, the players and the ball.

  5-6 St. Matthews Street, Rugby CV21 3BY

- **St. John the Baptist Church, Hillmorton,** is situated next to Hillmorton Locks. The oldest parts date from about 1240 but the church was extensively altered about 100 years later. The carved bosses on the roof crossbeams of the nave date from the 16th century, one having a 'green man' face. The mahogany pulpit was installed in 1779. The Royal Coat of Arms above the chancel arch is that of Queen Anne.

  Hillmorton Locks CV21 4PP

- **Braunston is an old canal town.** The local Canal Society has produced a useful leaflet for boaters which can be downloaded here: **http://www.braunston.org.uk/variable/organisation/29/attachments/ Braunston%20Canal%20Society%20Web%20Version.pdf**

- **Cropredy** is a small village that is, perhaps, best known for the huge outdoor folk music festival held here every August. Starting in 1978 as a small private performance to local people by the folk band Fairport Convention, it now attracts up to 20,000 visitors.

- **The Church of St. Mary the Virgin, Cropredy,** which lies at the bottom of a narrow lane in the centre of the village, dates from the 13th century with additions from the 14th and 15th. Some of the windows date from the 13th and 14th centuries. The very rare pre-Reformation brass lectern, which is in the form of an eagle, was hidden in the river during the Civil War and only recovered years later.

  Church Lane, Cropredy OX17 1PL

- **Banbury Museum,** which is situated next to the canal in the Castle Quay Shopping Centre, is devoted to the history of the town. There are displays on the Civil War, plush manufacturing, the Victorian market town and costume from the 17th century to the present day, together with exhibitions of work by local artists.
Castle Quay Shopping Centre, Spiceball Park Road, Banbury OX16 2PQ
- **Broughton Castle, Banbury,** is a moated and fortified manor house, mostly dating from the mid 16th century, although the earliest parts were built in 1306 and the gatehouse in the early 15th century. The great hall has 16th century windows and a mid 18th century plaster ceiling, while the dining room has double linenfold panelling dating from the mid 16th century. The King's Chamber and Queen Anne's Room were used by James I and his wife, Anne. The chapel was consecrated in 1331 and the altar and encaustic floor tiles date from then.
Banbury OX15 5EB
http://www.broughtoncastle.com/
- **Soldiers of Oxfordshire (SOFO), Woodstock,** opened in 2014 and has displays including a recreated Great War trench and a mock up section of a Horsa Glider from D Day. Themes include 'the 21st century soldier', the frontline, Winston Churchill and the Queens Own Oxfordshire Hussars, prisoners of war, and the liberation of Bergen-Belsen by the Oxfordshire Yeomanry.
Park Street, Woodstock OX20 1SN
http://www.sofo.org.uk/
- **Blenheim Palace.** Built in the early 18th century to celebrate victory over the French in the War of the Spanish Succession. Blenheim is the home of the Duke of Marlborough and was the birthplace of Sir Winston Churchill. The state rooms contain paintings, tapestries and furniture, and there is a permanent Churchill exhibition. Named a World Heritage Site, there are over 2000 acres of parkland and gardens designed by Capability Brown. Other attractions include a miniature train, a giant hedge maze, a butterfly house and an adventure playground.
Woodstock OX20 1PP
http://www.blenheimpalace.com/
- **Oxford University,** the oldest university in the English speaking world, is made up of 38 independent colleges, many of which open their quads,

gardens and chapels to visitors (times of opening are shown on the porter's lodge of each college). Some colleges also open their dining halls - that of Christ Church was used in the Harry Potter films as Hogwarts' great hall.

- **The Ashmolean Museum** was founded in 1683 and houses world famous collections ranging from Egyptian mummies to contemporary art, representing most of the world's great civilisations, and containing objects dating from 8000 BC to the present day. Of particular note are the collection of Raphael drawings, the most important collection of Egyptian pre-Dynastic sculpture and ceramics outside Cairo, the only great Minoan collection in Britain, outstanding Anglo-Saxon treasures, the foremost collection of modern Chinese painting in the Western world, and a collection of over 300,000 coins, currency and medals . There are also European paintings, drawings, prints, sculpture and musical instruments from the Middle Ages to the present day and Eastern ceramics, sculpture, metalwork, paintings and prints.
Beaumont Street, Oxford OX1 2PH
http://www.ashmolean.org/

- **The Bodleian Library** offers guided tours of its historic rooms including the 15th century Divinity School, the mediaeval Duke Humfrey's Library, and the Radcliffe Camera.
Broad Street, Oxford OX1 3BG
http://www.bodleian.ox.ac.uk/whatson/visit

- **The Story Museum** celebrates the world of stories with exhibitions aimed at both children and adults.
Rochester House, 42 Pembroke Street, Oxford OX1 1BP

- **Oxford Castle** is a large Norman castle, much of which was destroyed in the Civil War. By the 18th century the part that remained had become a prison. This was expanded in 1876 and eventually closed in 1996. The mediaeval remains are grade I listed. Guided tours allow visitors to explore the 900 year old crypt, the 18th century Debtors' Tower and Prison D-Wing and the mound of the 11th century motte and bailey castle, as well as St. George's Tower, which offers panoramic views of Oxford.

- **The University Church of St. Mary the Virgin** has one of the most beautiful spires in England and an eccentric baroque porch. The 13th century tower offers views across the city.

High Street, Oxford OX1 4BJ

http://www.university-church.ox.ac.uk/

- **The Church of St. Mary Magdalen.** Built in 1194 to replace a Saxon wooden church that had burnt down, it was remodelled in 1841–42 by George Gilbert Scott, becoming the first Victorian Gothic interior in Oxford.

  Magdalen Street, Oxford OX1 3AE

  http://www.stmarymagdalenoxford.org.uk/

- **The Oxford University Museum of Natural History** houses collections of zoological, entomological, geological, palaeontological and mineralogical specimens, accumulated in the course of the last three centuries.

  Parks Road, Oxford OX1 3PW

  http://www.oum.ox.ac.uk/

- **The Pitt Rivers Museum** has outstanding collections from many cultures around the world and three floors of display cabinets showing masks, magic, musical instruments and much more. It is reached through the Museum of Natural History.

  Parks Road, Oxford OX1 3PW

- **The Museum of the History of Science** has an unrivalled collection of historic scientific instruments housed in the world's oldest surviving purpose-built museum building.

  Broad Street, Oxford OX1 3AZ

  http://www.mhs.ox.ac.uk/

- **Christ Church Picture Gallery.** An important collection of Old Master paintings and drawings, owned by Christ Church College and housed in a purpose-built gallery.

  Oriel Square, Oxford OX1 4EP

  http://www.chch.ox.ac.uk/gallery

- **The Bate Collection of Musical Instruments** has one of the most magnificent collections of musical instruments in the world. Over 1000 Western orchestral instruments from the renaissance up to modern times are on display.

  St. Aldate's, Oxford OX1 1DB

  http://www.bate.ox.ac.uk/

THE PEAK FOREST CANAL

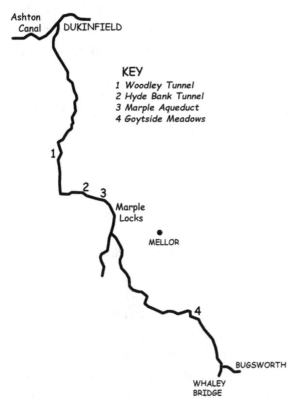

KEY
1 Woodley Tunnel
2 Hyde Bank Tunnel
3 Marple Aqueduct
4 Goytside Meadows

Although less than 15 miles long, the Peak Forest Canal is one of the country's most scenic waterways, running through stunning countryside to the edge of the Peak District. For much of its length, it runs alongside the River Goyt. Starting at Dukinfield Junction in Greater Manchester, where it connects with the Ashton Canal, it runs southwards to end at Bugsworth (sometimes spelled Buxworth) in Derbyshire.

It is made up of two level stretches (or pounds) separated by the Marple Flight of 16 locks which, over the course of a mile, raise the canal by 209 feet. The two pounds are sometimes referred to as the Lower Peak Forest Canal and the Upper Peak Forest Canal, the epithets 'Lower' and 'Upper' referring to their height above sea level not their relative positions, since the Lower section is north of the Upper section.

In the Lower section there are two tunnels, the 176 yard long Woodley Tunnel and the 330 yard long Hyde Bank. Both tunnels are quite narrow and neither is wide enough for boats to pass each other (although the Hyde Bank looks as though it could be). So it's essential to make sure that each tunnel is clear before you move into it.

The Lower Peak Forest Canal forms part of the Cheshire Ring, together with the Macclesfield (which it meets at the top of the Marple Locks), the Trent & Mersey and the Bridgewater Canals. The Peak Forest's only branch splits off just three quarters of a mile before it reaches Bugsworth and runs for half a mile to Whaley Bridge.

A handcuff key is needed for Bridges 1 (Stanley Lift Bridge), 22 (Turflea Lift Bridge) and 24 (Wood End Lift Bridge) and the latter two also need a windlass to open them. A CRT key is needed for Bridges 25 (Higgins Clough Swing Bridge) and 30 (Carr Swing Bridge).

If you are approaching the Marple Locks towards the end of the day, it's important to ensure that you have enough time to get through them, as you are not allowed to moor within the flight itself.

In passing: things to see and do

Places of note:

- **Marple Aqueduct.** Situated just before the Marple Flight of locks, this was built in 1801 and is grade I listed.
- **Lock cottages.** The cottage next to Marple Bottom Lock was built in 1835 and that by Lock 9 in 1834.
- **Goytside Meadows Nature Reserve** consists of 25 acres between the canal and the River Goyt and is known for its wide array of wild flowers. It can be accessed from the canal towpath.
  Goytside Meadow Nature Reserve, Goytside SK22 4PS
- **Bugsworth Basin** was once the largest and busiest inland port on the British narrow canal network, where lime, limestone and gritstone from the Derbyshire quarries was transferred to narrowboats to be taken further afield. It was active until the 1920s and is now a scheduled ancient monument. Near the shop run by the Peak Forest Canal Company is a cabin displaying photographs, artefacts and models that tell the history of the canal, tramway and Bugsworth village.
  http://www.bugsworthbasin.org/

Places to visit:

- **Mellor Iron Age Fort.** Discovered in the 1990s, this Iron Age settlement was occupied from the Bronze Age to the Romano-British period. Excavations have revealed a spectacular hillfort that was founded in the Iron Age by the Celtic Brigantes tribe, although archaeological evidence shows that the site was occupied as long ago as 8000 BC. An Iron Age roundhouse has been reconstructed at Mellor by archaeology students from a local college.

- **St. Thomas's Church, Mellor,** stands close to the hill fort site. Its earliest parts date from the 15th century but it was remodelled and restored in the 18th and 19th centuries. It has a carved stone font which probably dates from the 11th century, a 700 year old pulpit and, in the churchyard, the end posts of the old village stocks, together with a sundial made from the remains of a late mediaeval cross.

Church Road, Mellor SK6 5LX

THE ROCHDALE CANAL

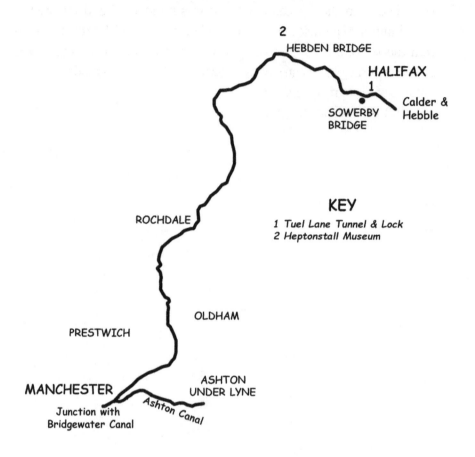

A trip along this broad canal has been described as "an exhausting but exhilarating journey with stunning views". It begins at Sowerby Bridge where it meets the Calder & Hebble Navigation and runs for 32 miles across the Pennines to Manchester where it joins the Bridgewater Canal at Castlefield Basin. Unlike the Leeds & Liverpool and the Huddersfield Narrow Canals which tunnel under the Pennine moors, the Rochdale goes over the top, through a staggering 91 locks. Originally, it had one more but, in 1996, Locks 3 and 4 were replaced by the Tuel Lane Lock, which is the deepest canal lock in England.

Just before Tuel Lane Lock comes the canal's only tunnel, the 114 yard long Tuel Lane Tunnel. Both lock and tunnel are controlled by a lock keeper and boats should only enter the tunnel once the lockkeeper has signalled that the lock is ready. Passage through the lock and across the summit pound is restricted and needs to be booked at least 24 hours in advance through the CRT local office (ring 03030 404040 during office hours).

The Rochdale forms part of several rings:
- the Cheshire Ring with the Macclesfield, Trent & Mersey, Bridgewater, Ashton and Peak Forest Canals
- the South Pennine Ring with the Huddersfield Broad, Huddersfield Narrow and Ashton Canals and the Calder & Hebble Navigation
- and the North Pennine Ring with the Bridgewater and Leeds & Liverpool Canals, and the Aire & Calder and Calder & Hebble Navigations.

The canal travels through a wide variety of scenery from crags and woods, to moorland, and from little villages and small towns to the city of Manchester.

In passing: a place to visit
- **Heptonstall Museum** tells the story of the surrounding area from prehistoric times until the present, including the counterfeiters and murderers known as the Cragg Vale Coiners, and Heptonstall's Parliamentarian garrison during the Civil War. The museum is housed in the old Heptonstall Grammar School building which dates from 1771 and some of whose original features have been carefully preserved. Church Yard Bottom, Heptonstall HX7 7PL

THE SHROPSHIRE UNION CANAL

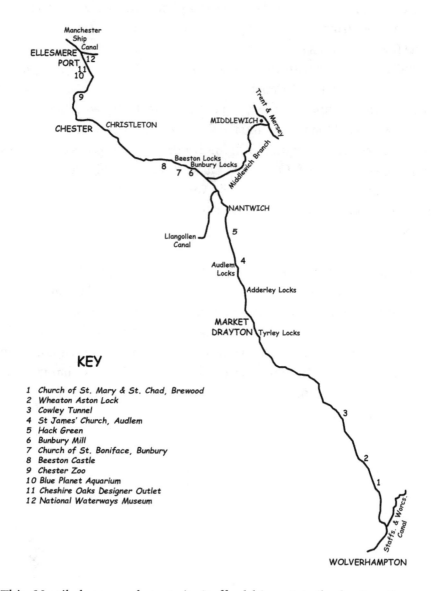

KEY

1 Church of St. Mary & St. Chad, Brewood
2 Wheaton Aston Lock
3 Cowley Tunnel
4 St James' Church, Audlem
5 Hack Green
6 Bunbury Mill
7 Church of St. Boniface, Bunbury
8 Beeston Castle
9 Chester Zoo
10 Blue Planet Aquarium
11 Cheshire Oaks Designer Outlet
12 National Waterways Museum

This 66 mile long canal starts in Staffordshire, at Autherley Junction, runs through Shropshire, and ends at Ellesmere Port in Cheshire. Its upper end links with the River Mersey and the Manchester Ship Canal and its lower end with the Staffordshire & Worcestershire Canal and, through this, to the entire Birmingham Canal Navigations. It also has links with the Llangollen Canal, and has two branches, the quarter mile long Dee Branch which links to the River Dee and the 10 mile long Middlewich Arm. The latter (sometimes known as the 'New Cut') runs across farmland, ending in a short built up stretch near its junction with the Trent & Mersey at Middlewich. Together with the main line of the Shropshire Union, the Staffordshire & Worcestershire Canal and the Trent & Mersey Canal, it forms the Four Counties Ring.

The Shropshire Union, which was completed in 1835, was one of the last British canals to be built. Much of it runs through open countryside and it travels over a number of aqueducts and through the 81 yard long Cowley Tunnel at Gnosall.

There are 47 locks but also some long lock-free stretches, the longest being the 17½ miles stretch between Wheaton Aston (the second lock on the canal) and the Tyrley Flight of five locks at Market Drayton. After this, there are several more flights - the five Adderley Locks which come 4¼ miles after Tyrley, and then, a mile further on, the fifteen Audlem Locks, which are spread over a distance of a mile and a half. Further up the canal (after the Middlewich Arm has left) there is a set of six locks in the space of 2¾ miles. The first two of these, the Bunbury Locks, form a staircase. The fourth and fifth, which are both wide locks, are known as Beeston Stone Lock and Beeston Iron Lock. The Stone Lock, which is built entirely of blocks of sandstone, will let two boats in abreast without problems. However, the Iron Lock, which is made from cast iron plates riveted and bolted together has started to bulge inwards and nowadays CRT recommends that only one boat goes through at a time.

The Middlewich Branch travels mostly through open countryside. It has four locks, which are widely spaced. Be very careful if you approach the Shropshire Canal by way of the Middlewich Branch - it's a blind exit.

In passing: places to visit
- **The Church of St. Mary the Virgin and St. Chad, Brewood** (pronounced 'Brood'). The chancel dates back to the 13th century, the north aisle to the 14th and the rest of the church was rebuilt in the 15th century. Extensive restoration was carried out in the late 19th century. There are interesting monuments and memorials from the 16th and 17th centuries.
  Church Road, Brewood ST19 9BT
- **Market Drayton** is a pretty market town with half-timbered buildings dating from the 17th and 18th centuries. It claims to be the 'home of

gingerbread', which has been produced there for over 200 years. The Wednesday street market has been held for more than 750 years.

- **St. Mary's Church, Market Drayton.** The oldest part of this stone-built church is the Norman doorway, dated 1150. There is some fine stained glass. Church Street, Market Drayton TF9 1AD
- **Market Drayton Museum** tells the story of the town and surrounding villages from the earliest times to the present day.
  53 Shropshire Street, Market Drayton TF9 3DA
- **St. James' Church, Audlem,** was founded in the mid 13th century. The lower walls of the chancel and nave date from the 14th century. The clerestory windows and panelled ceiling were installed in Tudor times. The pulpit dates from 1609. Major restorations took place in the 19th and 20th centuries.
  The Square, Audlem CW3 0AH
- **Hack Green** was one of the first WWII radar stations which, in the 1950s, was transformed into a secret nuclear bunker. Declassified in 1993, the 35,000 square foot underground bunker is now open to visitors. A short walk from the canal, it is signposted from Bridge 86 (Hack Green Bridge). French Lane, Nantwich CW5 8AP
  http://www.hackgreen.co.uk/
- **Nantwich** is a pretty market town with black and white half-timbered buildings.
- **St. Mary's Church, Nantwich,** has been described as a "magnificent building". The chancel and the stone pulpit date from the 14th century. There are intricately carved choir stalls and some unusual stone carvings. Church Lane, Nantwich CW5 5RQ
- **Nantwich Museum** tells the story of the town through the ages, including Roman salt making, the Great Fire of Tudor times, the Battle of Nantwich (1644) and the more recent shoe and clothing industries. There are also displays of clocks and paintings.
  Pillory Street, Nantwich CW5 5BQ
  http://nantwichmuseum.org.uk/
- **Dorfold Hall, Nantwich,** is a grade I listed house, built between 1616 and 1621, which retains its original plaster ceilings and oak paneling. The beautiful gardens contain a magnificent chestnut tree which is believed to be over a thousand years old.

Chester Road, Nantwich CW5 8LD

http://www.dorfoldhall.com/index.html

- **Bunbury Mill.** A restored mid 19th century working watermill. Guided tours offer visitors the chance to try their hand at weighing, winnowing and grinding wheat, and testing flour quality.

  Mill Lane, Bowes Gate Road, Bunbury CW6 9PY

  http://www.bunburymill.com/

- **The Church of St. Boniface, Bunbury.** Built in 1320, this church boasts an impressive chancel and chantry as well as a 14th century alabaster tomb with graffitti carved during the Civil War by prisoners held in the church. Also to be seen are a carved 14th century reredos, a series of mediaeval painted panels and an ornate monument commemorating Admiral Sir George Beeston who fought against the Spanish Armada.

  Vicarage Lane, Bunbury CW6 9PE

- **Beeston Castle.** Built in the 1220s and now in ruins, Beeston incorporates the banks and ditches of an Iron Age hillfort. It stands on a hill 500 feet above the Cheshire plain, with views extending for 30 miles in every direction.

  Chapel Lane, Beeston CW6 9TX

- **Christleton.** A pretty little village with timber framed almshouses. Winner of the Best Kept Village Award in 2011.

- **Chester Wall.** This is the most complete town wall in Britain, and offers a two mile circular walk. Begun in the 1st century, it was added to over the years, and was probably completed in the 12th century. It is now a scheduled ancient monument.

- **Chester Rows** are unique half-timbered covered walkways on two levels, along four of the main shopping streets, Bridge Street, Watergate Street, Eastgate Street and Northgate Street. No one has been able to explain satisfactorily why they were built in this way. Originating in the 13th century, it seems that the individual galleries only started to be linked together to form continuous walkways in the 14th century. While some of the original buildings remain, some of the facades are Victorian copies.

  Chester CH1 1NG

- **Chester Cathedral.** Founded as a Benedictine abbey in 1092, the church was added to and rebuilt from the mid 13th century. It has some of the best preserved monastic buildings in the country. The lady chapel dates from

the 13th century, and the south transept and superbly carved choir stalls from the 14th. The monks' refectory has a complete stone wall-pulpit. The free standing sandstone and Welsh slate bell tower was erected in 1975.
Abbey Square, Chester CH1 2HU
https://chestercathedral.com/

- **Chester Falconry & Nature Gardens** opened in 2015 and is home to twelve birds of prey including a golden eagle, kestrel, barn owl and vulture. Bird displays take place 7 days a week.
  12 Abbey Square, Chester CH1 2HU

- **The Grosvenor Museum** tells the story of Chester, with displays including impressive collections of silver, art, geology and Roman tombstones, as well as a townhouse illustrating home life from the 17th century to the 1920s.
  27 Grosvenor Street, Chester CH1 2DD
  http://grosvenormuseum.westcheshiremuseums.co.uk/

- **The Roman Amphitheatre, Chester,** was built around 100 AD and is the largest stone-built Roman amphitheatre in Britain. Artefacts found here during a huge archaeological excavation in 2005 are housed in the Grosvenor Museum.
  Vicar's Lane, Chester CH1 2HS

- **Dewa Roman Experience** offers an interactive insight into the city in Roman times and also includes archaeological excavations of Roman, Saxon and mediaeval remains.
  1-2 Bridge Street, Chester CH1 1NL
  http://www.dewaromanexperience.co.uk/

- **The Church of St. John the Baptist, Chester,** was founded as the great Saxon Minster of Mercia in AD 689 but was rebuilt in 1075 as the Cathedral and Collegiate Church of Chester, a title it retained until the Reformation in 1541. Possibly one of the oldest churches in Europe that is still in use, it is a grade I listed building and has fine Norman and Early English features.
  Vicar's Lane/Little St. John Street, Chester CH1 1SN

- **Cheshire Military Museum** tells the story of the soldiers of Cheshire from the 17th century to the present day. Displays include uniforms, weapons, medals, and a typical trench of the WWI Western Front. There are also trophies of war, including the alabaster chair of the Amir of Scinde, captured in 1843 by the 22nd Regiment of Foot.
  The Castle, Chester CH1 2DN

- **Chester Zoo,** which covers 125 acres, has 20,000 animals from 500 exotic and endangered species.
  Moston Road, Upton, Chester CH2 1EU
- **Blue Planet Aquarium** is the largest in the UK.
  Longlooms Road, Cheshire Oaks, Ellesmere Port CH65 9LF
  https://www.blueplanetaquarium.com/
- **Cheshire Oaks Designer Outlet** is the largest of its kind in Europe, with 145 shops selling luxury and high street brands at a considerable discount.
  Kinsey Road, Ellesmere Port CH65 9JJ
  http://www.mcarthurglen.com/uk/cheshire-oaks-designer-outlet/en/
- **The National Waterways Museum** tells the story of the canals and the people who worked on them, with a display ranging from boats to canal company buttons. Four original dock workers' cottages are furnished to represent different periods from the 1840s to the 1950s.
  South Pier Road, Ellesmere Port, CH65 4FW
  https://www.boatmuseum.org.uk/

THE STAFFORDSHIRE & WORCESTERSHIRE CANAL

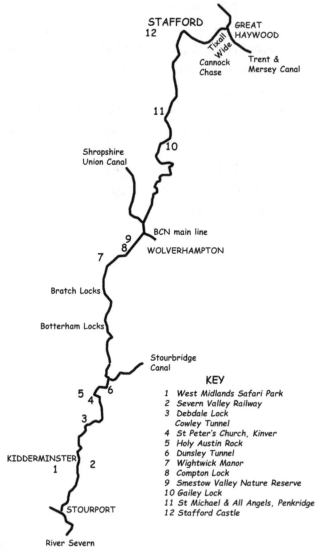

The Staffs. & Worcs., as it is commonly known, is 46 miles long, and runs from Stourport in Worcestershire (where it links with the River Severn) to Great Haywood (where it meets the Trent & Mersey Canal). It has a total of 43 locks and connects to the Stourbridge Canal, the Birmingham Canal Navigations and the Shropshire Union Canal. With the Shropshire and the Trent & Mersey Canals it forms the Four Counties Ring (the counties in question being Cheshire, Shropshire, Staffordshire and the West Midlands) while, with the Stourbridge, Dudley, and the Worcester & Birmingham Canals, the Birmingham Canal Navigations and the River Severn it forms the Stourport Ring.

In the five mile section immediately south of the junction with the Stourbridge Canal, the Staffs. & Worcs. travels between steep sandstone banks and through two short tunnels - the 65 yard long Cookley Tunnel and the even shorter Dunsley Tunnel. The Cookley Tunnel is unusual because it goes under part of the village.

There are some longish flat stretches on the Staffs. & Worcs., the longest being between Compton and Gailey Locks (Locks 31 and 32) a distance of just over 10 miles. The only flights of locks are the Botterham staircase of two locks and the three Bratch Locks which were originally built as a staircase but now have a few feet between consecutive locks. The Bratch Locks usually have a lock keeper on duty during the summer.

Just north of the junction with the Shropshire Union Canal, near Wolverhampton, there is a half mile long narrow cutting which is not wide enough for boats to pass each other. There are passing places and the rule is the same as that for cars on the road - the boat that gets to the passing place first pulls in and waits for the other to pass.

Most of the canal's course is rural, although it runs through Kidderminster, Penkridge and a number of villages.

In passing: things to see and do

Places of note:

- **Next to Debdale Lock** is a small cave where, so it said, the navvies who built the canal used to shelter.
- **Next to the Bratch Locks** is an 18th century octagonal toll house, now used by the lock keeper.
- **Compton Lock** is believed to be the first lock ever to have been built by James Brindley, the engineer of this and a number of other canals. All his early canals were 'contour canals' which wove around taking advantage of the natural contours of the land, rather than following more direct routes that would entail building locks.
- **The 19th century roundhouse at Gailey** originally enabled the toll keeper to watch the boats on the canal, but is now used as a shop.
- **Cannock Chase.** The northern part of the canal runs through the open heathland and pine woods of Cannock Chase.
- **Tixall Wide is a popular place for mooring.** The canal was deliberately widened here at the request of the owner of Tixall Hall who objected to having an industrial canal in his grounds and wanted it to look more like an ornamental lake. It is home to many water birds. The 16th century Tixall Gatehouse (all that remains now of Tixall Hall) can be seen in the distance.

Places to visit:

- **Stourport** is an interesting Georgian town which was built as an inland port and is the only town in Britain that arose as the result of the building of a canal.

- **West Midlands Safari Park, near Kidderminster,** has numerous attractions including penguins, sea lions, lorikeets, meerkats and hippos, an African Village with pygmy goats and lemurs, the UK's largest animatronic Dinosaur attraction, and guided bus tours.
  Spring Grove, Bewdley DY12 1LF
  http://www.wmsp.co.uk/

- **The Severn Valley Railway** is a full-size standard-gauge railway line that runs regular, mainly steam trains over the 16 miles between Kidderminster and Bridgnorth in Shropshire. Passengers can get off at Highley to visit the Engine House and the Visitor Centre.
  Comberton Hill, Kidderminster DY10 1QX
  http://www.svr.co.uk/Default.aspx

- **The Church of Saint Peter, Kinver,** dates back to the 11th century but there is some evidence of a Saxon church on the site. The nave roof is early Norman with a double collar beam truss and barrel vaulting. The tower dates from 1380.
  Church Hill, Kinver DY7 6HX

- **Holy Austin Rock** is a huge outcrop southwest of the village of Kinver, in the cliffs known as Kinver Edge. Cave dwellings were built into the sandstone, possibly in the 8th century and, 1000 years later, were still being used as homes. A book of 1777 describes them as "curious, warm and commodious and the garden extremely pretty". Six families were recorded as living there in 1830. After becoming a tourist attraction in the early 1900s, they were abandoned by the middle of the 20th century. Now restored by the National Trust, they are thought to have been the inspiration for Tolkien's Hobbit holes.

- **Wightwick Manor** (pronounced 'Wittick') is a grade I listed manor house which was both built and furnished under the influence of the Arts and Crafts movement. Completed in 1893, it has original William Morris wallpapers and fabrics, De Morgan tiles, Kempe glass and a fine collection of Pre-Raphaelite art. It has been owned by the National Trust since 1937.
  Wightwick Bank, Wolverhampton WV6 8BN

- **Smestow Valley Local Nature Reserve** is home to over 55 species of breeding bird including buzzards, snipes, reed buntings and lesser spotted woodpeckers. There are also great crested newts, badgers, Daubenton bats and otters. By Bridge 61 (Tettenhall Old Bridge).
Meadow View Terrace, Wolverhampton WV6 8NX
- **Bantock House Museum** is surrounded by formal gardens and 43 acres of parkland. In its oak panelled rooms it has displays of decorative glass, tiles, painted enamels, japanned ware, cut steel jewellery, toys, dolls, porcelain, Pre-Raphaelite paintings and Arts and Crafts period furnishings.
Finchfield Road, Wolverhampton WV3 9LQ
http://www.bantockhouse.co.uk/
- **The Church of St. Michael and All Angels, Penkridge,** dates from the 13th century. The tower and porch were added in the 14th century. Additional modifications were made in the 16th century. The present nave roof was installed in the 1880s, incorporating six oak angels from the original 16th century roof.
New Road, Penkridge ST19 5DN
- **The Ancient High House, Stafford,** is said to be the largest surviving Tudor timber framed town house in England. Opened as a museum in 1986, it has an extensive collection of period furniture and architectural features representing various periods in its history. It is also home to the Staffordshire Yeomanry Museum.
Greengate Street, Stafford ST16 2JA
- **Shire Hall Gallery** is a grade II* listed building which contains a Victorian Crown Court, complete with holding cells where prisoners awaited trial. The gallery itself hosts art and craft exhibitions throughout the year, as well as activities for all ages.
Market Square, Stafford ST16 2LD
- **St. Chad's Church, Stafford,** is the oldest building in the town and is grade II* listed. It was built in the 12th century and restored in the mid 19th century by, among others, George Gilbert Scott. It has a wealth of interesting carvings.
Greengate Street, Stafford ST16 2HP
- **Stafford Castle.** Built by William the Conqueror, the site extends over 26 acres and consists of keep, inner bailey, outer bailey, woodland and

herb garden. There is a visitor centre with artefacts from archaeological excavations, a scale model of the motte and bailey castle and an audio-visual area.

Newport Road, Stafford ST16 1DJ

THE STOURBRIDGE CANAL

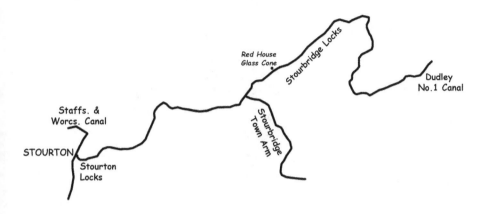

The Stourbridge Canal is less than six miles long and has 20 locks. It begins at Stourton and ends at Black Delph, just below the Delph Bottom Lock, where it meets the Dudley No. 1 Canal head on. Its importance nowadays is that it links the Staffordshire & Worcestershire Canal to its west with the BCN to its east and forms part of the Stourport Ring. However, it was built originally to service the local glass industry which, at the time, was world famous for its cameo glass and cut crystal. In the 19th century there were more than 20 glassworks in this area.

The locks are divided into two flights - the Stourton four which come immediately after the junction with the Staffordshire & Worcestershire, and the Stourbridge sixteen. Between the two flights is a stretch of 1¾ miles, towards the end of which the canal crosses the River Stour via a short aqueduct. Once the flight is past, the canal runs for just under 3½ miles to its junction with the Dudley No. 1 Canal, below the Delph Bottom Lock.

The canal has one branch - the Stourbridge Town Arm - which is slightly over a mile long and has no locks. It leads to moorings and a grade II listed bonded warehouse which, having been restored from a derelict condition, now has a new role as a community facility.

In passing: a place to visit
- **Red House Glass Cone.** Situated between Locks 12 and 13, the cone was built at the end of the 18th century. It remained in continuous use until 1936 and now is one of just four glass-making cones left in the UK. It offers

exhibitions telling the story of glass-making in the area, and has displays of glass wares spanning over 100 years, as well as demonstrations of glass making.

High Street, Wordsley DY8 4AZ

THE STRATFORD-UPON-AVON CANAL

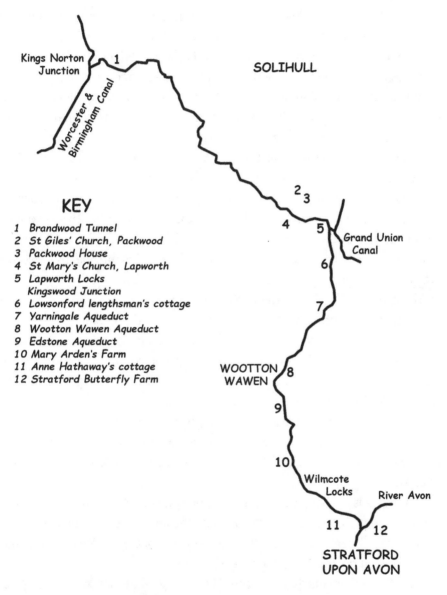

Kings Norton Junction

Worcester & Birmingham Canal

SOLIHULL

Grand Union Canal

WOOTTON WAWEN

Wilmcote Locks

River Avon

STRATFORD UPON AVON

KEY

1 Brandwood Tunnel
2 St Giles' Church, Packwood
3 Packwood House
4 St Mary's Church, Lapworth
5 Lapworth Locks
   Kingswood Junction
6 Lowsonford lengthsman's cottage
7 Yarningale Aqueduct
8 Wootton Wawen Aqueduct
9 Edstone Aqueduct
10 Mary Arden's Farm
11 Anne Hathaway's cottage
12 Stratford Butterfly Farm

This canal runs for 25½ miles and is usually described as consisting of two sections. The northern section runs from King's Norton in Birmingham (where it meets the Worcester & Birmingham Canal) to Kingswood (or South Lapworth) Junction, where the quarter-mile long Kingswood Arm links it with the Grand Union Canal. The southern section runs between Kingswood

Junction and Stratford-upon-Avon, where it meets the River Avon. It has a total of 54 locks.

About a mile after leaving King's Norton, the canal passes through the 352 yard long Brandwood Tunnel, but the first lock is not encountered for another 10 miles. This is the start of the Lapworth Flight - and in the next six miles there are 36 locks. However, the six miles after that are interrupted by only a single lock. This stretch is followed by the Wilmcote Flight of eleven locks, and the last two miles or so of the canal presents a final six locks before the River Avon is reached.

Some of the locks (such as Lock 47 on the Wilmcote Flight) are especially narrow while others (such as Lock 15 at Lapworth) are quite short. All of these need additional care when manouevring boats in and out. There is only one broad beam lock - that between the canal and the River Avon. All the rest are narrow.

There are four aqueducts. Three of these - the Yarningale, the Wootton Wawen (pronounced 'Wootton Warn') and the Edstone, all of which are on the southern section of the canal - are made of iron and date from the 19th century. The first two are relatively short but the Edstone, at just over 158 yards, is the longest in England (although not, of course, in Britain, that record being held by the 336 yard long Pontcysyllte Aqueduct on the Llangollen Canal). There are also a number of roving bridges across the canal, including two over the Lapworth Flight.

Once past the suburbs of Birmingham, the canal travels through pleasant open countryside, with the occasional small village, before ending in the Stratford Basin, next to the River Avon and the Shakespeare Memorial Theatre.

Bridge 2 is a swing bridge which is normally left open. The Shirley Draw Bridge (Bridge 8), which comes soon after the aqueduct over the River Cole, is electrically operated and needs a CRT key to work it. Bridges 26 and 28 (a drawbridge and a lift bridge) need a windlass.

The canal forms part of the Avon Ring, together with the River Severn, Worcester & Birmingham Canal and the Birmingham Canal Navigations.

In passing: things to see and do

Places of note:

- **King's Norton Stop Lock.** Coming almost immediately after the junction with the Worcestershire & Birmingham Canal, this guillotine-gated lock is grade II* listed. Its function is not to raise or lower the canal but to regulate the flow of water between the two canals. This was important when different canals were owned by different companies, but is less so today and this lock gate hasn't been used for over 50 years. It is therefore permanently left open.
- **Brandwood Tunnel.** Parts of the handrail used by boatmen to pull their boats through the tunnel can still be seen.
- **Lowsonford lengthsman's cottage.** The barrel-roofed cottage next to Lock 31 dates from around 1812 and was built for the 'lengthsman' whose job was to maintain both the lock and the next stretch of canal. Such cottages are rare, although originally there were six between Lapworth and Preston Bagot. Acquired by the Landmark Trust in 1992, it is rented out as a holiday cottage.

Places to visit:

- **Packwood House.** This National Trust property was originally built in the 16th century, but its interiors were extensively restored in the 1920s and 1930s. It contains a fine collection of 16th century textiles, needlework and furniture and the Carolean garden has a famous collection of yew trees. Packwood Lane, Lapworth B94 6AT
- **The Church of St. Giles, Packwood,** is a short walk from Packwood House and dates in part to the late 13th century. The west tower - added in the late 15th century by the Lord of Baddesley Clinton as a penance for a murder he had committed - is known as the Tower of Atonement. The font is 12th century and was discovered being used as a watering trough for animals at a local farm. There are fragments of mediaeval stained glass, an 18th century carved screen and a fragment of a wall painting dating to the 14th century. The chancel screen and the benches in front of the choir pews are 15th century. Glasshouse Lane, Packwood B94 6PU
- **The Church of St. Mary the Virgin, Lapworth.** This is a grade I listed building dating from around 1100 but with additions from the following three centuries. Church Lane, Lapworth B94 5NX

- **Wootton Wawen** has many historic buildings including the stone-built Palladian style Wootton Hall which dates from the 1680s, the 16th century Bull's Head Inn, several timber framed houses and the early 18th century Manor Farm.
- **St. Peter's Church, Wootton Wawen,** is the oldest church in Warwickshire, with the tower probably dating from the 10th century or earlier. The east window is 14th century, the pulpit and choir screen 15th century, and there is a small chained library of 17th century theological works . The Lady Chapel houses an exhibition exploring Wootton's past, including how it got its name.

  Stratford Road, Wootton Wawen, B95 6BE
- **Mary Arden's Farm (or Mary Arden's House), Wilmcote.** Mary Arden was William Shakespeare's mother and, at different times, two separate grade I listed houses in Wilmcote have been said to have belonged to her. In 1930 one of these was bought by the Shakespeare Birthplace Trust and refurnished in the Tudor style. In 2000 it was discovered that it had actually belonged to Mary's neighbour, Adam Palmer, and it was renamed Palmer's Farm. Mary had lived nearby at Glebe Farm. Both houses and farm are now presented as a 'working Tudor farm'. The farm has a number of rare breeds, including pigs, sheep, cattle, goats and birds of prey.

  Station Road, Wilmscote CV37 9UN
- **Anne Hathaway's cottage** is a 500 year old thatched cottage situated in the village of Shottery just outside Stratford-Upon-Avon. It is said to have been the childhood home of Shakespeare's wife.

  Cottage Lane, Shottery CV37 9HH
- **Hall's Croft** was the home of Shakespeare's daughter, Susanna, and her husband, Dr John Hall, an eminent physician. Built in the 16th century it has Jacobean additions, and contains both furniture and paintings of the period and a small exhibition on early medicine.

  Old Town, Stratford-upon-Avon CV37 6BG
- **Holy Trinity Church, Stratford-upon-Avon,** was built in the 13th century and remains very much as it was in Shakespeare's day. The two storey porch dates from the 15th century as do the huge doors bearing a knocker to be used by those seeking sanctuary. The Lady Chapel has a tomb which has been described as the finest Renaissance tomb in England. The chancel was

built in 1480 and the stalls and misericords (carved with images of birds, beasts, demons and people) have been in continuous use for over 500 years. The mediaeval font is probably where Shakespeare was baptised. A 1611 first edition of the King James Bible is on display in the chancel. Shakespeare and members of his family are buried in the chancel.

Old Town, Stratford-upon-Avon CV37 6BG

- **Shakespeare's birthplace.** William Shakespeare inherited this house in 1601 on the death of his father, who had been Mayor of Stratford. It later became an inn. It was bought by the Shakespeare Birthplace Trust in 1847.

Henley Street, Stratford-upon-Avon CV37 6QW

- **Stratford Butterfly Farm.** The largest tropical butterfly display in the UK. Over 250 species of tropical butterfly from 20 different countries and a huge selection of tropical plants in a landscaped greenhouse. There are also two South American green iguanas and a number of (non-insect-eating) birds including Indian ring necked parakeets, African mousebirds and Chinese painted quail.

Swans Nest, Stratford-upon-Avon CV37 7LS

http://www.butterflyfarm.co.uk/attraction/index.php

THE TRENT & MERSEY CANAL

The Trent & Mersey Canal is 93 miles long and runs from Derbyshire (where it joins the River Trent) to Cheshire (where it meets the Bridgewater Canal). It was one of the first canals in the country, being opened in 1777. For most of its length it is a narrow canal but its extremities - the section east of Burton-upon-Trent and the section above the Middlewich Junction - are wide.

For the sake of clarity, we have illustrated it with two sketch maps, one for the more southerly section between Shardlow and Great Haywood and the second for the section north of Great Haywood.

TRENT & MERSEY CANAL - SOUTHERN SECTION

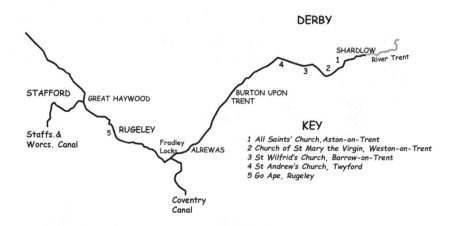

DERBY

SHARDLOW
River Trent

STAFFORD   GREAT HAYWOOD

BURTON UPON TRENT

Staffs.& Worcs. Canal   RUGELEY

Fradley Locks   ALREWAS

Coventry Canal

KEY

1 All Saints' Church, Aston-on-Trent
2 Church of St Mary the Virgin, Weston-on-Trent
3 St Wilfrid's Church, Barrow-on-Trent
4 St Andrew's Church, Twyford
5 Go Ape, Rugeley

The canal has 75 locks and four tunnels. The tunnels are all in the final 32 miles of the canal, with three of them in the final seven. The first to be reached, (the Harecastle Tunnel, just south of Kidsgrove) is also the longest, at 2919 yards. It needs careful navigation as the level of the roof varies (although most of the changes are indicated by yellow reflecting paint). However, an experienced boater drowned here some years ago after knocking his head on the roof and falling in, so this is probably one of the places where it's a good idea to wear a life jacket. Also, unlike many other tunnels, this was built without ventilation shafts - not a problem in the days before diesel but now necessitating airtight gates at the tunnel end and a fan system to remove fumes. This makes the passage through the tunnel quite noisy.

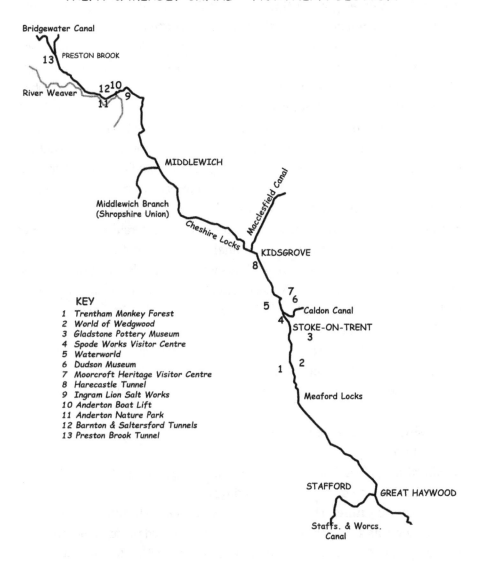

Bridgewater Canal

13 PRESTON BROOK

River Weaver 12 10 9 11

MIDDLEWICH

Middlewich Branch
(Shropshire Union)

Cheshire Locks

Macclesfield Canal

KIDSGROVE

8

KEY
1 Trentham Monkey Forest
2 World of Wedgwood
3 Gladstone Pottery Museum
4 Spode Works Visitor Centre
5 Waterworld
6 Dudson Museum
7 Moorcroft Heritage Visitor Centre
8 Harecastle Tunnel
9 Ingram Lion Salt Works
10 Anderton Boat Lift
11 Anderton Nature Park
12 Barnton & Saltersford Tunnels
13 Preston Brook Tunnel

7
6 Caldon Canal
5 4 STOKE-ON-TRENT
3

1 2

Meaford Locks

STAFFORD GREAT HAYWOOD

Staffs. & Worcs.
Canal

The Barnton Tunnel (a short distance after the canal connects to the River Weaver via the Anderton Boat Lift) is 572 yards long. The Saltersford Tunnel, coming hot on the heels of the Barnton, is 424 yards long. It has a kink in it because tunnelling was carried out from both ends and didn't meet smoothly in the middle. Finally, the Preston Brook Tunnel, which was the first major canal tunnel to be built, is at the very end of the canal, and is 1239 yards long.

The Barnton, Saltersford and Preston Brook Tunnels are limited to one-way traffic and there are set times for northbound and southbound vessels. In the winter, passage through the tunnels may need to be booked.

Many of the locks are well-spaced but there are a few short flights, such as the five Fradley Locks and the four Meaford Locks, as well as the notorious flight of 25 Cheshire Locks which, in more recent times, has been dubbed 'Heartbreak Hill'. This, however, is not because of the length of the flight but because the spacing is uneven, making it hard to establish a rhythm of working. Some are paired locks - they were built like this in the 19th century to reduce congestion - but many of the 'duplicates' have fallen into disrepair.

The Trent & Mersey has links with a number of other waterways. At its start, it meets the River Trent. At Fradley it links to the Coventry Canal, and at Great Haywood to the Staffordshire & Worcestershire. Just north of Stoke on Trent, it meets the Caldon Canal and, after another 5½ miles, the Macclesfield Canal. At Middlewich it links with the Middlewich Branch of the Shropshire Union Canal. The Anderton Boat Lift links it to the River Weaver, and its northern end makes an end-on junction with the Bridgewater Canal inside the Preston Brook Tunnel.

It forms part of two rings - the Four Counties Ring with the Shropshire Union and the Staffordshire & Worcestershire Canals, and the Cheshire Ring with the Ashton, Peak Forest, Bridgewater and Macclesfield Canals.

In passing: things to see and do

Places of note:

- **Shardlow** is Britain's most complete surviving example of a canal village and has over 50 grade II listed buildings.
- **Harecastle Tunnel.** There are, in fact, two tunnels. The first, built by James Brindley, was 2880 yards long and boats were legged through. But this was a very slow process and a second, wider tunnel with a towpath was built to speed things up. This is the tunnel that remains in use (the first is gated off). At 2926 yards, it is the fourth-longest navigable canal tunnel in the UK.
- **The Anderton Boat Lift** was opened in 1875 to move boats up and down the 50 feet between the River Weaver and the Trent & Mersey Canal by means of two huge water tanks with watertight doors. The world's first boat lift, it was in operation until 1983, when it was closed. However, it was fully restored in 2002 since when it has been back in use.

Places to visit:

- **Shardlow Heritage Centre.** Housed in the salt warehouse, which is the oldest canal building in Shardlow, the Centre has displays on themes including boatbuilders, the coming of the Trent & Mersey Canal, the Shardlow Boat Company, the North Staffordshire Railway Company and local public houses and breweries. There is a full size replica of a narrowboat back cabin as well as rural craft tools, farming implements and information on the Aston to Shardlow tramway.
The Wharf, Shardlow DE72 2GA,

- **Derby Cathedral.** The 16th century tower is one of the tallest in England. A family of peregrine falcons has nested here for many years and is often seen. Although founded in the 10th century, the main body of the church dates from 1725. There is an 18th century wrought iron rood screen.
Iron Gate, Derby DE1 3GP
http://www.derbycathedral.org/

- **Derby Museum & Art Gallery** has the largest collection in the world of paintings by the 18th century artist, Joseph Wright, a large porcelain display, an exhibition of weaponry and militaria, an Egyptian mummy and much else.
The Strand, Derby DE1 1BR

- **Derby Silk Mill** is a UNESCO World Heritage Site and stands on the site of the world's first factory. It tells the story of how the secrets of spinning silk were stolen from Italy and brought to Derby.
Silk Mill Lane, Derby DE1 3AF

- **Pickford's House.** An 18th century townhouse, furnished and decorated as it would have been at the time. Reception rooms, bedrooms and kitchens are on view. There is also a 1940s air raid shelter in the basement as well as a fine collection of toy theatres.
41 Friar Gate, Derby DE1 1DA

- **All Saints' Church, Aston-on-Trent,** is a grade I listed building dating from the 12th century, with later additions. As well as evidence of Anglo-Saxon stonework, it has a Norman tower, a 13th-15th century nave and chancel, and the remains of a Celtic preaching cross.
Shardlow Road, Aston-on-Trent DE72 2DH

- **The Church of St. Mary the Virgin, Weston-on-Trent,** is a grade I listed building dating from the 12th century. The Harpur Chapel has effigies from the 15th-17th centuries. Many of the interior features, including the pulpit, date from the 17th century.

Swarkestone Road, Weston-on-Trent DE72 2DR

- **St. Wilfrid's Church, Barrow-upon-Trent,** dates from the mid 13th century and was restored in the 19th century. It was, at one time, an outpost for the Knights Hospitallers of St. John.

  Church Lane, Barrow-upon-Trent DE73 7HB

- **St. Andrew's Church, Twyford,** is a grade I listed building dating from the 12th century and built by the Knights Hospitallers of St. John for the use of travellers crossing the Trent. It has a 13th century chancel, the remains of mediaeval wall painting and a Jacobean altar rail.

  Ferry Lane, Twyford DE73 7HJ

- **The National Brewery Centre Museum** tells the story of the Bass family and their role in the development of brewing.

  Horninglow Street, Burton-upon-Trent DE14 1NG,

  http://www.nationalbrewerycentre.co.uk/

- **All Saints' Church, Alrewas,** is a grade I listed building. The oldest parts are 12th century but much of it dates from the 13th, 14th and 16th centuries. The font is from the 15th century and the pulpit from the 17th.

  Church Road, Alrewas DE13 7BT

- **The National Memorial Arboretum** in Alrewas opened in 2001 to "honour the fallen, recognise service and sacrifice, and foster pride in our country". It has over 50,000 trees and nearly 300 memorials for the armed forces, civilian organisations and voluntary bodies who have served the country. At 11am every day in the Millennium Chapel, there is two minutes silence, followed by the Last Post and Reveille and then an introductory talk about the arboretum.

  Croxall Road, Alrewas DE13 7AR

  http://www.thenma.org.uk/

- **Go Ape** is a tree top adventure with nearly 1500 metres of tree-to-tree crossings, zip wires, Tarzan swings, rope ladders and a variety of obstacles and crossings. Suitable for adults and children.

  Birches Valley Forest Centre Car Park, Rugeley WS15 2UQ

  https://goape.co.uk/days-out/cannock

- **Trentham Monkey Forest.** An opportunity to watch 140 Barbary macaques living in total freedom in 60 acres of forest.

Stone Road, Trentham ST4 8AY

http://monkey-forest.com/

- **World of Wedgwood,** just by the canal at Barlaston, has a museum telling the story of Wedgwood ceramics, and offers tours of the factory.
  Wedgwood Drive, Barlaston ST12 9ER
  https://www.worldofwedgwood.com/
- **Gladstone Pottery Museum, Longton.** Housed in a Victorian pottery factory, it tells the story of the potteries with original workshops, bottle ovens, a tile gallery, and an exhibition on the history of the flushing toilet. There are demonstrations of pottery making and the opportunity to make a piece for yourself.
  Uttoxeter Road, Longton ST3 1PQ
- **Spode Works Visitor Centre, Stoke-on-Trent.** Housed in the former Spode pottery, the birthplace of bone china, there are displays relating to its history, from the 1770s to 2008 when it closed. There are demonstrations of china painting and printing with original copperplates.
  Elenora Street, Stoke-on-Trent ST4 1QQ
- **Waterworld** is billed as the UK's top water theme park.
  Festival Park, Etruria, Stoke-on-Trent ST1 5PU
  http://www.waterworld.co.uk/
- **Dudson Museum** - see listing under Caldon Canal
- **Moorcroft Heritage Visitor Centre, Burslem,** offers displays of Moorcroft pottery, a grade II listed bottle oven and the opportunity to tour the factory.
  Sandbach Road, Burslem ST6 2DQ
- **Ingram's Lion Salt Works, Marston,** is a restored historic open-pan salt making works, and was the last place in Britain to have produced salt by evaporating brine. Situated next to the canal, the museum opened in 2015.
  Lion Salt Works, Ollershaw Lane, Marston CW9 6ES
  http://lionsaltworks.westcheshiremuseums.co.uk/
- **Anderton Lift Visitor Centre** is next to the Lift itself and has an interactive exhibition.
- **Anderton Nature Park** has many unusual plants, as a result of the lime-rich waste created by the local salt and soda ash industries. In June and July there are spectacular displays of orchids. Over 11 miles of paths and cycle routes.
  Lift Lane, Anderton, Northwich CW9 6FW

THE UNION CANAL

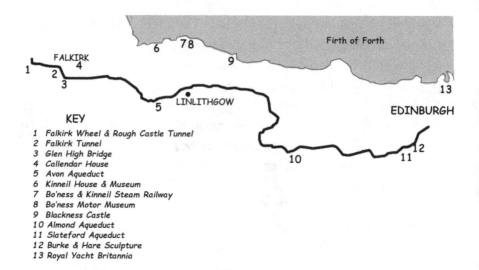

KEY
1 Falkirk Wheel & Rough Castle Tunnel
2 Falkirk Tunnel
3 Glen High Bridge
4 Callendar House
5 Avon Aqueduct
6 Kinneil House & Museum
7 Bo'ness & Kinneil Steam Railway
8 Bo'ness Motor Museum
9 Blackness Castle
10 Almond Aqueduct
11 Slateford Aqueduct
12 Burke & Hare Sculpture
13 Royal Yacht Britannia

This Scottish canal runs from Falkirk (where it meets the Forth & Clyde at the Falkirk Wheel) to Edinburgh. It is 31 miles long and has several aqueducts but no locks. Originally there was a flight of locks between the two canals but these fell into disrepair in the 1930s and the Union Canal itself was closed to navigation in the 1960s. In 2001, the Union Canal was reopened and the two canals were reunited the following year by means of the Falkirk Wheel, which has since become a major tourist attraction.

The aqueducts include the Avon Aqueduct near Linlithgow (which, at 270 yards long, is the second longest in the UK), the Almond Aqueduct near Ratho (142 yards) and the Slateford Aqueduct (167 yards) in Edinburgh. All three were built in the early 19th century and retain their original structure.

This canal has some notoriously tight bends approaching bridges - especial care needs to be taken when circumnavigating these.

In passing: things to see and do
Places of note:
- **The Falkirk Wheel** - see the description in the introductory section on the Forth & Clyde Canal.
- **The Falkirk Tunnel** is cut through bare rock and stalagtites have formed in places. It is the only rock tunnel in Scotland.

- **Glen High Bridge** (Bridge 61) is known as the 'Laughin' & Greetin' bridge' from the two faces carved into it - a laughing face on one side and a sad face on the other. ('Greet' is the old Scottish word for 'weep'.)
- **Between Bridges 4 & 5** (Meggetland Old Bridge and Kingsknowe Road Bridge) is a 12 foot high sculpture carved from an elm tree by Robert Coia. It depicts Burke and Hare, the Victorian mass murderers who, earlier in their lives, were navvies working on the Union Canal.

Places to visit:
- **Callendar House and Park** is a 14th century, French chateau-style house with a working (and interactive) kitchen dating from 1825. There is a section of the Roman Antonine Wall (a UNESCO World Heritage site) in the park.
Callendar Road, Falkirk FK1 1YR
- **The Antonine Wall** was built around AD 142 and stretched across the country from the River Clyde to the River Forth. It was built mostly out of layers of turf, to a height of 10 feet, with a ditch nearly 16 feet deep. There were 17 forts and a number of smaller 'fortlets' along its length.
- **Kinneil House, Kinneil Museum and James Watt's cottage.** The house is the historic home of the Dukes of Hamilton and dates back to the 15th century. Its rare renaissance wall paintings are said to be the best in Scotland. There is a section of the Antonine Wall and a Roman 'fortlet' in the grounds. The museum is housed in the 17th century stable block and tells the story of the estate from Roman times to the present day. The cottage, to the rear of the house, dates from the 18th century, and is where inventor James Watt worked on the development of the steam engine. It is now semi-derelict. The museum is open most days but the house has limited opening hours.
Bo'ness EH51 OPR
https://kinneil.wordpress.com/
- **Bo'ness & Kinneil Steam Railway** offers a 10 mile round trip on a steam train along the Forth Estuary. The associated Museum of Scottish Railways is housed in three large buildings and includes a wide variety of exhibits from full size locomotives to antique railway signs.
Bo'ness Station, Union Street, Bo'ness EH51 9AQ
http://www.bkrailway.co.uk/

- **Bo'ness Motor Museum** houses a small private collection of TV and film cars, props and memorabilia including the Lotus Esprit SI from *The Spy Who Loved Me*, the BMW 750 from *Tomorrow Never Dies*, and Tardis props from *Dr Who*.
  Bridgeness Road, Bo'ness EH51 9JR
  http://www.motor-museum.bo-ness.org.uk/
- **St. Michael's Parish Church, Linlithgow,** dates mostly from the mid 15th century with extensive 19th century restorations.
  The Cross, Linlithgow EH49 7AL
  http://www.stmichaelsparish.org.uk/home
- **Linlithgow Palace,** now preserved as a ruin, was one of the main residences of Scottish monarchs in the 15th and 16th centuries. James V and his daughter Mary Queen of Scots were both born here. The adjacent loch is a Site of Special Scientific Interest.
  Kirkgate, Linlithgow, EH49 7AL
  https://www.historicenvironment.scot/visit-a-place/places/linlithgow-palace/
- **Linlithgow Canal Centre Museum** is the only canal museum in Scotland. Housed in a former canal stable, it has displays illustrating the history of the Edinburgh & Glasgow Union Canal, together with boat models and artefacts from the working life of the canal.
  Manse Road Basin, Linlithgow EH49 6AJ
  http://www.lucs.org.uk/
- **Blackness Castle.** This 15th century fortress was used as a location in the TV series Outlander. It has served as a royal castle, a garrison fortress, a state prison and an ammunition depot. It is often described as "the ship that never sailed" because, from the seaward side, it looks like a stone ship. The foreshore and mudflats to the east of the castle are part of the River Forth Site of Special Scientific Interest, and provide an important feeding area for overwintering birds.
  Blackness, Linlithgow EH49 7NH
  https://www.visitscotland.com/info/see-do/blackness-castle-p248561
- **Edinburgh Castle** is the number one visitor attraction in Scotland. It is built on top of an extinct volcano and offers spectacular views of the city. It holds the Stone of Destiny, an ancient symbol of Scottish monarchy that, from 1296 to 1996 was part of the English monarch's coronation throne.

Also on display are the Scottish crown jewels, which date from the 15th and 16th centuries. St. Margaret's Chapel, built around 1130, is Edinburgh's oldest building. The huge gun known as Mons Meg was given to James II of Scotland by Duke Philip of Burgundy in 1457 and was among the most powerful guns in mediaeval Europe.

- **The Scottish National War Museum** is housed in a former ordnance storehouse at Edinburgh Castle. It was built in the 1700s and later used as a military hospital. It contains a large collection of militaria.
- **The Regimental Museums** in the New Barracks of Edinburgh Castle pay homage to the Royal Scots Dragoon Guards and other Scottish regiments. Pride of place is given to the eagle and standard of the 45th French infantry, captured at the Battle of Waterloo.
  Castlehill, Edinburgh EH1 2NG
  http://www.edinburghcastle.gov.uk/
- **Edinburgh Zoo** has over 1000 animals, including flamingos, koalas, penguins, chimpanzees - and the UK's only giant pandas.
  134 Corstophine Road, Edinburgh EH12 6TS
  http://www.edinburghzoo.org.uk/
- **Camera Obscura.** Opened in 1835, this is the oldest visitor attraction in Edinburgh. It offers an interactive opportunity to see the city in a completely different way.
  Castlehill, Edinburgh EH1 2ND
  http://www.camera-obscura.co.uk/
- **The National Museum of Scotland** offers a wide range of exhibits and interactive displays. Collections include art, design & fashion, natural history, Scottish history, science & technology, and 'world cultures'.
  Chambers Street, Edinburgh EH1 1JF
  http://www.nms.ac.uk/national-museum-of-scotland/
- **The National Galleries of Scotland.** Comprising the Scottish National Gallery, the Scottish National Portrait Gallery and the Scottish National Gallery of Modern Art.
  Scottish National Gallery, The Mound, Edinburgh EH2 2EL
  Scottish National Portrait Gallery, 1 Queen Street, Edinburgh EH2 1JD
  Scottish National Gallery of Modern Art, 75 Belford Road, Edinburgh EH4 3DR
  https://www.nationalgalleries.org/

- **The Museum of Childhood** houses a huge range of toys from the 18th to the 21st centuries. Other exhibits include rattles, cod liver oil bottles, school slates and clothing, from christening robes to fancy dress.
  42 High Street, Edinburgh EH1 1TG
  http://www.edinburghmuseums.org.uk/Venues/Museum-of-Childhood
- **The Palace of Holyroodhouse** is the Queen's official residence in Scotland. The state apartments, including the throne room and the morning drawing room, where the Queen gives private audiences, are open to the public, as are the chambers of Mary Queen of Scots and the site of the murder, by her husband, of her secretary, David Rizzio. There are fine plasterwork ceilings, an unrivalled collection of Brussels tapestries, and numerous works of art.
  Canongate, Edinburgh EH8 8DX
  http://www.royalcollection.org.uk/visit/palace-of-holyroodhouse
- **The Queen's Gallery,** housed in the Palace of Holyroodhouse, was opened in 2002 and hosts a programme of changing exhibitions from the Royal Collection.
  Canongate, Edinburgh EH8 8DX
  http://www.royalcollection.org.uk/visit/the-queens-gallery-palace-of-holyroodhouse
- **The Scottish Parliament.** Opened in 2004, the complex building (hailed as one of the most innovative designs in Britain today) is constructed from steel, oak, and granite.
  Horse Wynd, Edinburgh EH99 1SP
  http://www.scottish.parliament.uk/visit-and-learn.aspx
- **The Royal Botanic Garden, Edinburgh,** offers over 70 acres of landscaped grounds, a Victorian Temperate Palm House (the tallest of its kind in Britain), the Queen Mother's Memorial Garden and 'Windows on the World', a glasshouse experience offering the opportunity to explore the flora of ten distinct climatic zones.
  Arboretum Place, Edinburgh EH3 5NZ
  http://www.rbge.org.uk/the-gardens/home
- **The Royal Yacht Britannia** was used by the Royal Family for over 40 years but is now permanently moored at Leith. You can explore the five main decks, the bridge, the state apartments, the crew's quarters and the engine room, and visit the Royal Sailing Exhibition.
  Ocean Terminal , Leith EH6 6JJ
  http://www.royalyachtbritannia.co.uk/

THE WORCESTER & BIRMINGHAM CANAL

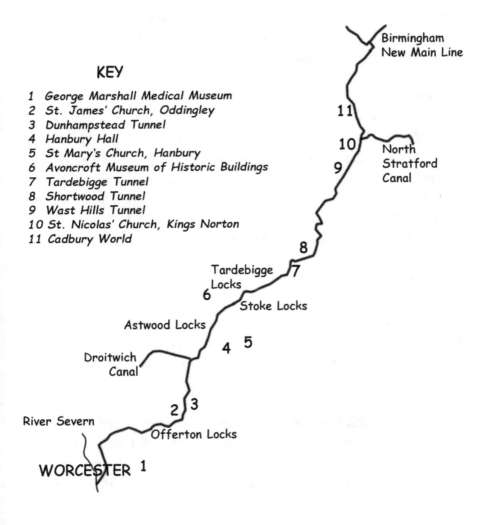

KEY

1 George Marshall Medical Museum
2 St. James' Church, Oddingley
3 Dunhampstead Tunnel
4 Hanbury Hall
5 St Mary's Church, Hanbury
6 Avoncroft Museum of Historic Buildings
7 Tardebigge Tunnel
8 Shortwood Tunnel
9 Wast Hills Tunnel
10 St. Nicolas' Church, Kings Norton
11 Cadbury World

This 29 mile long canal, unsurprisingly, starts in Worcester and ends in Birmingham. It has 58 locks, of which 30 form the grade II listed Tardebigge Flight, one of the longest lock flights in Europe. However, to compensate for the work of getting through the locks, there are some beautiful views from here! The Tardebigge top lock has a rise of fourteen feet, making it one of the deepest locks on the English canal system. There are three other, much shorter, flights - the Offerton (6), Astwood (5) and Stoke (6) - but, hard on the heels of the Stoke Flight comes the Tardebigge Flight.

There are five tunnels - the Dunhampstead Tunnel (230 yards long), the Tardebigge (580 yards), the Shortwood (614 yards), the Wast Hills (2726 yards - just over a mile and a half) and the Edgbaston (105 yards).

The Worcester & Birmingham Canal meets the BCN in Birmingham and the River Severn in Worcester and links with the northern section of the Stratford-upon-Avon Canal at King's Norton, and the Droitwich Canal at Hanbury.

Together with the River Severn, the Staffordshire & Worcestershire Canal, the Stourbridge Canal, and the Dudley, Netherton Tunnel Branch and New Main Line Canals of the BCN, it forms the Stourport Ring. With the Stratford Canal, BCN and the Rivers Severn and Avon it forms the Avon Ring. And with the Droitwich Canal and the River Severn it forms the short Droitwich Ring.

Much of the canal's route is through pretty countryside.

In passing: things to see and do

Places of note:

- **Lock 4 (Blockhouse Lock)** offers a good view of Worcester Cathedral.
- **The red brick toll house** opposite the junction with the North Stratford Canal (King's Norton Junction), was built in 1802 and is grade II listed.

Places to visit:

- **The Greyfriars, Worcester,** is a timber-framed merchant's house built in 1480. It was rescued from demolition after WWII and was carefully restored with period furniture, tapestries and other decorative pieces. The floor in the entrance hall was rescued from Wychbold Hall, Droitwich, which was being demolished. The Greyfriars is now owned by the National Trust.
  Friar Street, Worcester WR1 2LZ
- **Worcester Cathedral,** built in the late 11th century, has Royal tombs, mediaeval cloisters, an early 12th century chapter house and superb Victorian stained glass. The cathedral library - which holds the second largest collection of mediaeval manuscripts of any cathedral in the UK - is open by appointment.
  Worcester WR1 2LA
  http://www.worcestercathedral.co.uk/

- **Worcester Guildhall** was built in 1722 by a pupil of Sir Christopher Wren. The iron gates and railings facing the High Street were erected in 1750. The Assembly Room was remodelled in 1791 and again in 1877 when the ornate Italianate painted ceiling was installed. There is a good collection of paintings.
  High Street, Worcester WR1 2EY
- **St. Swithun's Church, Worcester.** Originally mediaeval, this church was completely renovated in 1733 apart from the west tower. The interior is entirely Georgian with box pews, a west gallery, and a triple-decker pulpit. The organ, dating from 1795, is grade I listed. The church is no longer in use and is cared for by the Churches Conservation Trust.
  Church Street, Worcester WR1 2RH
- **The Commandery** is a grade I listed half-timbered Tudor house that was used as the Royalist headquarters before the final battle of the Civil War in 1651. In one of the rooms there are some impressive early wall paintings. The Commandery now houses a museum of local history, including displays relating to the Worcestershire Regiment and the Worcestershire Yeomanry Cavalry.
  Sidbury, Worcester WR1 2HU
  https://www.worcestershire.gov.uk/museums/info/1/the_commandery
- **The Museum of Royal Worcester** houses the finest and most extensive collections of Worcester porcelain, dating from 1751 to the present day. There is an audio tour by Antique Roadshow's Henry Sandon.
  Severn Street, Worcester WR1 2ND
  http://www.museumofroyalworcester.org/
- **Worcester City Art Gallery & Museum.** Housed in a beautiful Victorian building, there is wide range of exhibits including a gallery which tells the story of the Worcestershire Regiment and the Worcestershire Yeomanry Cavalry.
  Foregate Street, Worcester WR1 1DT
  http://www.museumsworcestershire.org.uk/museums/site/index.php
- **The Infirmary Museum** offers an interactive exhibition exploring the history of one of England's oldest infirmaries.
  University of Worcester, City Campus, Worcester WR1 3AS
  https://medicalmuseum.org.uk/the-infirmary/
- **The Worcester Museum of Freemasonry** holds large collections of glass and ceramics and masonic medals and jewels as well as masonic

regalia and 'masonic curiosities' including trivets, horse-brasses and meerschaum pipes.

The Masonic Hall, Rainbow Hill, Worcester WR3 8LX

http://www.worcestermasonicmuseum.co.uk/

- **The George Marshall Medical Museum** tells the story of the development of modern medicine, with a particular focus on Worcester. There is a collection of rare medical books, some dating back to the 17th century, a collection of death masks, thought to be from prisoners executed in the early 19th century at Worcester gaol, and a collection of Royal Army Medical Officer's equipment and uniforms dating from the Boer War.

Charles Hastings Education Centre, Worcester Royal Hospital, Charles Hastings Way, Worcester WR5 1DD

https://medicalmuseum.org.uk/georgemarshallmuseum/

- **St. James' Church, Oddingley,** dates mostly from the 15th century, although the tower was added in the 17th. It was extensively restored in the mid 19th century.

Church Lane, Oddingley WR9 7NE

- **Hanbury Hall** can be reached by a walk across the fields from Lock 40 (Astwood Bottom Lock). Built in the first decade of the 18th century, it is set in 400 acres of gardens and parkland. It has collections of fine porcelain, silver and paintings, and a staircase whose walls are painted with scenes from Greek mythology. It is now owned by the National Trust.

School Road, Droitwich WR9 7EA

- **St. Mary's Church, Hanbury,** is a grade I listed building dating from 1210. It was altered in the 14th century, extensively rebuilt in Georgian times, and heavily restored in 1860 and now reflects the styles of all these periods. The south chapel contains some fine monuments. There are Georgian box pews and a musicians gallery.

Astwood Lane (off School Road), Hanbury B60 4BP

- **Avoncroft Museum of Historic Buildings.** Over 30 historic buildings spanning 700 years have been rescued and brought here. They include a timber-framed medieval hall, a working windmill, a Victorian gaol, church, and toll cottage, traditional farm buildings - and the national collection of telephone kiosks, including Dr Who's Tardis.

Stoke Heath, Bromsgrove B60 4JR

http://www.avoncroft.org.uk/

- **St. Nicolas' Church, King's Norton.** The original 11th century church was rebuilt in the 13th century and again in the 14th when the south aisle and arcade were added. The south porch and doorway are 15th century. Major restoration work occurred in 1872. The building is now grade I listed.
  81 The Green, King's Norton B38 8RU
- **Cadbury World** offers self-guided tours through interactive displays on chocolate-making and the history of Cadbury's.
  Linden Road, Bournville B30 1JR
  https://www.cadburyworld.co.uk/

PART THREE - ONTO THE CANAL

PLANNING YOUR TRIP IN DETAIL
by John

You've chosen which canal you're going on. You've booked your boat. What then? Do you want to plan your trip or are you happy just to wait and see how it goes? We tend to plan on a day-to-day basis, with a general idea of where we want to get to before we have to turn around. But it's never set in stone because we never know what interesting places we might want to explore along the way, or how heavy the traffic will be at locks.

If you like to plan, however, it's not difficult to do so. The first thing you need to decide is how many hours you're going to spend cruising. You'll be unlikely to do much more than two hours on the first day of your holiday. Boats have to be cleaned and made ready after the previous users, so they're usually not ready till about 2pm and, by the time you've got everything on board and stowed away, and have had your compulsory training from the hire company staff, it can be mid-afternoon before you set off. Similarly, you're unlikely to do any cruising at all on the last day - unless you want to get up very early - because the hire company usually needs the boat to be returned by 9am.

As to the rest of the trip, don't be tempted to over-estimate your cruising hours. If you do, it could result in you having to get up early in order to get on your way each day, missing out on the pleasure of a leisurely lunch sitting on the canal bank in the middle of the countryside, and possibly missing out on a good mooring place at the end of the day. On a busy canal, most of the decent places can be taken by mid afternoon. Remember too that, although narrowboating is about doing things in a leisurely way, it's also quite strenuous, so you need time to relax at the end of the day, otherwise you'll find you're tired out at the end of the holiday - which rather defeats the object of the exercise.

Once you've worked out the available hours for the week, multiply the number by three. This will give you the total number of miles you can manage, so if you're going 'out and back' rather than doing a ring, you'll need to halve it to know how far you can go before you have to turn back. However, this result doesn't take locks and bridges into account. Going through a lock can take between ten and twenty minutes, depending on whether the lock is for you (and you can go straight in) or against you (meaning you have to fill it or empty it before you can use it) and also on how many active people you have in your crew and whether there's a queue at the lock (which can happen when the canal is busy). So that needs to be factored into your calculations - as do swing and lift bridges. Although these should only take five or ten minutes to negotiate, they can affect your timing if there are more than one or two.

An easier way to work out your cruising plan, however, is to go to **http://www.narrowboats.org/canal_route_planner.aspx** There you will find a form to fill in. It asks, first, if you are a novice, intermediate or advanced. We suggest you put 'intermediate' because the website does seem to assume that beginners will be going very, very slowly. It then gives you the options of 'out and back', a one way trip, or a ring. After that, you put in the details of your holiday - the number of days, the hours you want to cruise each day, and the number of hours you'll cruise on the first and last days. Clicking 'continue' will bring you to a page where you fill in the name of your hire company and you can specify which marina you'll be going from. All you have to do then is to click on 'calculate trip' and you'll be given a list of options. However, the information about miles and number of locks that is given on the list of options can be a bit confusing. So we recommend clicking on all the 'select this trip' links in turn. You will then be shown a map of each route, with information about locks and miles for each section of the trip, and an indication of where you will need to turn round.

Possibly the simplest method of planning is to buy a copy of *Clegg's Canal Time Map* which shows the entire UK waterway network, divided into '2 hour' sections. It is available from the Inland Waterways Association (**https://www.waterways.org.uk/shop/**) for just a few pounds.

If you want to try cruising a ring, and you think you'd like to do about six hours a day (which allows you to have a leisurely breakfast, stop for lunch, and - hopefully - find a good place to moor at the end of the day) you need to plan carefully. Not including the first day and the last day, you will need at least:

- 22 days for the North Pennine (or Two Roses) Ring (Leeds & Liverpool Canal, Aire & Calder Navigation, Calder & Hebble Navigation, Rochdale Canal, Ashton Canal)

- 22 days for the Outer Pennine Ring (Ashton Canal, Huddersfield Broad Canal, Huddersfield Narrow Canal, Calder & Hebble Navigation, Aire & Calder Navigation, Leeds & Liverpool Canal, Bridgewater Canal, and Rochdale Canal)
- 15 days for the South Pennine (or Rochdale) Ring (Calder & Hebble Navigation, Huddersfield Broad Canal, Huddersfield Narrow Canal, Rochdale Canal)
- 12 days for the Four Counties Ring (Shropshire Union Canal, Trent & Mersey Canal, Staffordshire & Worcestershire Canal)
- 11 days for the Cheshire Ring (Bridgewater Canal, Ashton Canal, Peak Forest Canal, Macclesfield Canal, Trent & Mersey Canal)
- 11 days for the Warwickshire (or Midlands) Ring (Coventry Canal, Oxford Canal, Grand Union Canal, Birmingham Canal Navigations, Birmingham & Fazeley Canal)
- 9 days for the Black Country (or Staffordshire) Ring (Birmingham Canal Navigations, Staffordshire & Worcestershire Canal, Trent & Mersey Canal, Coventry Canal, Birmingham & Fazeley Canal)
- 6 days for the shorter Birmingham Ring (Birmingham Main Line Canal, Wyrley & Essington Canal, Daw End Branch Canal, Rushall Canal, Tame Valley Canal, Birmingham & Fazeley Canal)

Remember these are *cruising* days. So, as well as adding your start day and your end day to the total, you also need to factor in how much time you want to spend sightseeing along the way.

These aren't all the rings that there are, but most of the others include a stretch on a river and are thus more suitable for experienced boaters.

WHAT TO PACK
by Annie

Before you even start to pack, you need to make sure that all your bags can be folded up to be stowed away. Don't take suitcases or cardboard boxes - there'll be nowhere to put them.

Clothes

Take clothes that you feel comfortable in. A canal boat is not the place for dressing up and, even if you decide to eat in pubs in the evening, you probably won't want to change more than your shirt or blouse. Remember, too, that a canal boat is much more informal than a sailing boat - smart blazers and peaked caps are not required!

Make sure, though, that you take clothes for all temperatures! We went one year in April and, when we left home, the sun was shining and it was really warm. The weather forecast was good, too. But - as so often - it was wrong. By the second day the temperature had dropped and, even with the heating turned on in the boat, I was really cold. And I'd only taken a couple of light jumpers. I don't think I took my coat off all week!

If there is any chance of rain (in other words, at any time in this country) and you wear socks, take lots of spare pairs! And, since standing in the rain steering the boat with water trickling down your neck is MOST unpleasant, you will also need either a mac with a hood or a mac and a wide brimmed waterproof hat. The latter is preferable because a hood can restrict your vision and make turning your head awkward. John also takes a pair of waterproof over-trousers, in case of really foul weather.

Make sure you have some shoes with non-slip rubber soles. They don't have to be 'gym shoe' types with laces but they do need to be flat, stay on your feet and not slip. And have some shoes to change into when you aren't on the deck or you may find yourself traipsing mud through the boat.

Provisions

You also need to take food for at least two evening meals – you won't always be able to moor close to a decent pub. And, of course, you'll need food for breakfast every day, plus tea and coffee, milk and sugar. If you moor close to a village or town, there is often a supermarket where you can top up your supplies, but it's sensible to take enough food for a few lunches as well. If you're planning on cooking, don't forget the salt and cooking oil. You'll also need to take some sharp cooking knives - those supplied are almost invariably blunt.

If you're taking any tinned food that doesn't open with a ring pull, take a tin opener. The hire company should supply one but one year ours was so blunt it wouldn't work and John had to walk down to the next boat, about fifty yards away, carrying a tin of tuna, to ask if we could borrow theirs.

The fridge is likely to be very small with just a tiny freezing compartment. Don't take large bottles of milk because they won't fit. And, because you can't drink the tap water without boiling it first (which is fine if you want a cuppa but a bore if you just want a cold drink) take several large bottles of water.

We used to take some cheap sliced loaves to feed the ducks and swans along the way, because it's great fun. However, a few years ago, we learned that this is not a good idea. According to the RSPB, if the birds fill up on bread, it stops them from eating a balanced nutritious diet and they can become ill. The CRT warns that any bread left uneaten in or beside the canal can allow bacteria to breed and can attract rats. Fortunately, there are still things that are perfectly safe to feed to the ducks - and that they will enjoy just as much as bread. So you might like to stock up with some oats, sweetcorn and peas (tinned or frozen - as long as they're defrosted first!), lettuce or bird seed. Surprisingly, cooked rice is also fine. So if you have a takeaway one night and there's rice left over, you've got a nice breakfast to offer the ducks in the morning.

Other stuff

Take a portable airer to hang wet clothes on. You may not need it, but if it's very hot and you're needing to change clothes frequently and then wash them, or if it's raining and clothes get damp, you'll be pleased you did. They can usually be hung from the shower rail, although we have seen the occasional (moored) boat with the airer hung from the tiller. Take a small bottle of liquid soap as well, in case you need to wash clothes.

Take a couple of comfortable folding chairs and a few cushions. Depending on the design of the boat, you may need the chairs to sit out on the deck (and you'll need them anyway if you want to sit on the bank once you're moored). Narrowboats, in my experience, are not the most comfortable of places so extra cushions are worth taking. I always take a large cushion I can sit on together with a large black bin bag to put it in to keep it clean, and I sit on this on the deck as we're going along. It brings you very close to the water and gives you a new perspective of the canal . . . very peaceful. (But don't be tempted to dangle your hands in the water - there could be debris floating under the surface that could injure you.)

Take a can of air freshener. If it's hot, you may occasionally get a whiff from the loo towards the end of the week. It can cost up to £25 to have it pumped out, but if it's just the odd whiff, air freshener is a lot cheaper.

Don't forget to take the sun block. Even if it's not particularly sunny, you can be exposed to a lot of UV rays if you're steering the boat for hours on end (unless, of course, it's raining).

There's usually a shop at the marina so if you find you've forgotten something essential (such as toothpaste or soap) you can usually buy some.

Finally, take some empty yoghurt cartons. If you tie up using pins, which you may have to do out in the countryside, put a carton on the top of each pin so that people coming along the towpath can see them. A plastic water bottle with the top end cut off, or a white plastic bag tied tight, can also do this job.

Technology

Even if you're having a complete 'getting away from it all' holiday, you'll need your mobile 'phones. For a start, there's lots to photograph. But you'll also need them if one of the crew has to walk ahead to see whether a narrow stretch or a tunnel is clear and to let you know when it's safe to go through. And, of course, you'll also need it if you want to speak to someone from the hire company during your trip.

Then, if you've got a SatNav, take that, too. This may sound strange - after all, navigation on a canal is pretty straightforward! But it's very useful if you leave the boat. It will help you to find any of the attractions listed in Part Two. And, perhaps even more important, it will ensure that you don't get lost on your way back to the boat! On one occasion we stopped at Burton-on-Trent on the Trent & Mersey Canal. We walked into the town to find a supermarket. Eventually we found one and, loaded up with carrier bags, we started to walk back to the boat. but we couldn't remember which way we'd come. However, there were plenty of people around, so we stopped one and asked directions. To our surprise, he didn't know where the canal was. By the time the third person had claimed no knowledge of the whereabouts of the canal, we were feeling that we'd been transported into a parallel universe! Fortunately, we did eventually find someone who could direct us. But we were very tired by the time we got back.

Bicycles

Some of the attractions we've listed in Part Two are not within walking distance. For most of these you can catch a bus. But usually it's quicker to cycle. So, if you have bicycles, consider taking them with you. Check first with your hire company to see if they allow it, because the bikes will have to be carried on the roof of the boat. But, if you can take them, it can make visiting places much easier.

AT THE MARINA
by Annie

Once you have booked in, someone from the hire company will explain the workings of the boat to you. Inside the boat, you will be shown how to flush the loo (using a foot pedal and always with the lid shut to reduce the risk of odours), light the stove (holding the knob down for a few seconds after you've lit the gas to prevent it going out again) and pump out the water that remains in the tub after you've had a shower.

You should also be shown how to do your nightly checks (details of these are in the section on *Maintenance*), how to start and stop the boat and how to steer (more about this under *Cruising*). You will also need some training about locks - either by explaining it on a scale model, or (better still) taking you out to the nearest lock and helping you go through it. The first time we ever took a boat, we were given a video to watch - and that was it. It was totally inadequate and resulted in my being really scared of going through locks until we met some wonderful boat-owners who took time to show us how to do it and convinced us that locks could be fun! Make sure that you understand about locks before you're left in sole charge of the boat.

Before leaving the marina, you also need to know where to find the lifebelt, boat pole and gangplank (normally on the top of the boat), life jackets, torch and first aid kit (usually in one of the cupboards at the rear of the boat), the fire extinguisher and the fire blanket (often in the kitchen), and the mooring pins, hammer and windlass (usually in the cavity under the top step onto the deck). You also need to know how to work the navigation lights, where to find the horn and the bilge pump, and how to shut off the battery, gas and fuel. The cooker, fridge and heaters use bottled gas and the bottles (usually two of them) are to be found in a compartment at the front of the boat. You shouldn't need to do anything with them (unless it's to turn the gas off in an emergency) because once one is empty, a valve will automatically switch to the second bottle.

It's a good idea for all the crew to attend the briefing so that, if one forgets where something is or how to do something, someone else will remember.

CRUISING
by John

Setting off and steering

Unlike a car, a narrowboat won't start instantaneously. You have to turn the key (having first checked that the gears are in neutral) then wait a few seconds before firing the engine by turning the key the other way. Once you've started the engine, rev the motor slightly to ensure that the alternator is running. After this, you need to allow it a minute or two to warm up - but you can be casting off during this time. Untie your mooring ropes and put them tidily back on the deck or the roof. If you're on a river (although rivers aren't recommended for inexperienced boaters) always untie the downstream rope first. On a canal, it's best to untie the rope at the front first.

Always leave the ropes attached to the boat. And never leave them trailing - they could fall in the water and get tangled in the propeller, which could cause all kinds of problems.

Make sure that at least one person is on board the boat at all times when the engine is running. When the boat is untied, make sure you stow away the mooring pins - if one accidentally falls over the side because it's been left on the deck or on the roof, not only will you have to pay for it, but you could have problems mooring for the rest of your trip.

A narrowboat steers from the back and around a central pivot. So if you want to turn to the right, you need to push the tiller over to the left, and vice versa. It may seem odd at first, but it'll soon become second nature. To pull away from the bank, you need to get the front end out. Quite often, once you've untied the front, it will drift out. In that case, once the back's untied, the last person on shore should take a firm grip on the boat and give a steady push (to get the propeller into deeper water) while stepping aboard. You can then just edge forward gently (having first made sure that the way is clear). If the boat remains stubbornly aligned to the canal bank, one of the crew may need to push the front out, taking care not to fall in! The trick is not to push the boat *out* by leaning over the canal but to push yourself back onto the towpath. That way, if your feet should slip, you'll end up sitting on the bank, not splashing into the canal.

Sometimes the boat can be pushed against the bank by the wind or a current. In this case, pull your tiller right over towards the canal bank, put the boat into reverse and edge backwards very gently. Once the front is out, move into forward gear and you're away.

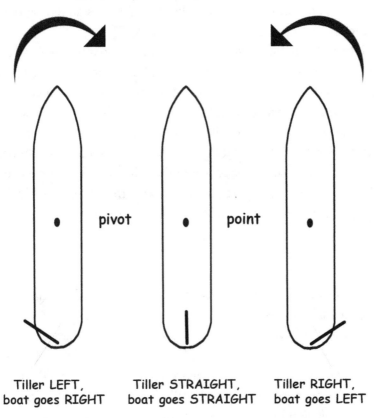

| Tiller LEFT, boat goes RIGHT | Tiller STRAIGHT, boat goes STRAIGHT | Tiller RIGHT, boat goes LEFT |

Manoeuvring and stopping

Unlike a car which has a wheel at each corner and can change direction rapidly, a narrowboat is much slower. When you move the tiller, it will be a moment or two before it takes effect. This has two consequences. Firstly, it makes it easy to oversteer - you move the tiller, nothing happens and so you move it further - and finish up further to the left or the right than you intended. So you need to be patient. Move the tiller and wait. If you find you haven't turned enough, then you can adjust your direction. This leads directly on to the second consequence of the narrowboat's slow response - you need to plan ahead. If you're in a car, you can swerve rapidly to avoid an obstruction, but in a narrowboat you need to manoeuvre well in advance. Of course, you'll be going much more slowly than you would in a car, as will all the other boats on the canal so, as long as you keep your eyes open, you shouldn't run into problems. (Don't worry about ducks or swans that suddenly swim out in front of you - they're old hands at getting out of the way at the last minute!)

This brings us to the question of stopping. How do you stop? A narrowboat doesn't have a brake pedal. The trick is to allow plenty of time (especially if there's a current and you're travelling downstream). Slow down to a crawl and, as you approach the place where you want to stop, go into neutral and then put the boat into reverse. Like everything else on a narrowboat, it will be a moment or two before it takes effect. If you need to, you can open the throttle to increase the engine revs and thus the braking effect when you're reversing. However, it's important to be aware that it's extremely difficult, if not impossible, to steer when you're in reverse gear. You may need an occasional short forward boost to get better control.

Cruising

On all waterways, the rule of the road is to drive on the right. On rivers and broad canals this is fairly easy. But on narrow canals (which is most of them), it can be quite shallow near the edges so it's best to steer down the middle and then move to the right when you see another boat coming towards you - and they should do the same. As you approach the boat, slow down - not only can going too fast literally rock the boat, but it's nice to have time to say hello and exchange a few words as you pass each other.

The usual speed limit on a canal is 4 miles an hour although it may be less (such as on stretches of the Montgomery Canal in Wales). And, even where the limit is 4 mph, you may need to go more slowly. The shallower and narrower the channel, the lower your top speed should be. A good way to judge whether you're going too fast is to watch your bow wave (the wave set up by the front of the boat), If it is hitting the bank, it means you're going too fast and could actually be causing physical damage to the canal bank. It is vital to slow down when passing moored boats - and that means right down to tick over, so your propeller hardly disturbs the surface of the water - as otherwise not only will you rock the boats and possibly dislodge their mooring pins but you will certainly get shouted at by anyone on board. At first, it may feel that you're crawling, but there should never be any need to hurry on a canal.

In any case, you should go very slowly for the first day or two, until you are feel confident in handling the boat. A narrowboat, being long, heavy and flat bottomed will keep going forward for a long time unless stopped (by going into reverse or by hitting something). It is amazing how fast things can happen at 4 miles an hour with several tons of boat! Make sure you are going slowly enough to avoid any problem which may be lurking round the next bend.

If you're in a narrow section of the waterway and pull to one side to let through a boat that's coming the other way, there is a chance - if the canal is particularly shallow - that you'll find yourself grounded. This happened to us a number of times on the Llangollen Canal some years ago. It was the height of summer and the canal was busy. Clearly a lot of the boaters were new to it and didn't know the rules of the road (they could have done with reading this book!) so, no matter what the situation, they pushed on through and we were the ones forced to give way. And because the sides of the Llangollen are very shallow in places (especially on the outside of bends), we kept getting grounded. However, although it's a nuisance, it's not a disaster. All you have to do (usually) is to reverse off. If that doesn't work, try pushing with a pole against the canal bank, while reversing gently. Make sure that the pole is at an angle (if you put it in vertically, it could break) and that you're standing so that, if the pole should slip, it doesn't hit you.

Bends

Sooner or later, you're going to reach a bend. Take it slowly and, if there are no boats coming towards you, stay in the middle of the channel. If another boat is coming and there's room, pull over to the right as you reach the bend (but not so far as to risk going aground). If you're not sure, stop and let the other boat come round first.

Sharp bends can be tricky with a long narrow craft and you may have to do a little shunting backwards and forwards in order to get round a tight turn. It's always safer to reverse a bit, manouevre and try again, rather than risk crashing into the bank.

Some canals have blind bends. If you're approaching one of these, give a five second blast on your horn. If you hear a response from a boat coming the other way, pull well over to the right and edge forward carefully.

If you're approaching another boat on a bend and there isn't room for you both to go round comfortably, it's usually easier for the boat using the inside of the bend to give way. But a general rule that we've always found to work is - if you're not sure, give way. Not only will you earn other boaters' gratitude but you'll avoid collisions.

If the boat coming towards you is a commercial boat, they should always be given right of way. Not only are they trying to earn a living, while you're just enjoying a holiday, but a laden boat needs all the depth of water it can get and its weight may make the boat less manoeuvrable.

Other canal users

You may well encounter canoes, rowing boats and other craft, as well as anglers on the bank. Give smaller boats plenty of room and ensure that you go very slowly if you're passing them - a strong wave from something the size of a narrowboat could easily cause them to collide with the bank or even overturn them.

As to anglers, slow down to tick over, in the same way as you would when passing moored boats, and keep well away from their side of the canal. Wait until you're at least one boat's length beyond the angler before starting to speed up again. Some anglers use very long rods that stretch across much of the canal. You may need to go into reverse momentarily to allow them time to draw their rods in. Once they've done so, you can use the middle of the channel - but remain in tick over.

Fishing clubs tend to meet at the weekends and, on Friday or Saturday nights, will put markers on the towpath to show which section of the canal they'll be using. If you see such markers, do not moor within - or even near - the markers unless you want to be woken at an early hour and told to beat it!

Bridges and narrow sections

When two boats are approaching a bridge or a narrow section of canal (such as an aqueduct), the one closer to it has priority. However, other factors may need to be taken into consideration. The position of moored boats or other obstructions may make it more practical for the boat further away to go through first, as may the strength of the wind or the direction of the current. Decide early on the correct course of action and, as always, if in doubt, give way.

If you signal to the other boat to come through first, make sure its crew can see you clearly. Use your whole arm and a big sweeping movement so they know exactly what it is that you're telling them.

Most of the bridges you'll encounter will be simple arch-type bridges, but you will also come across some swing and lift bridges. These should always be left as you found them - unless another boat has just come through and has left the bridge open for you, in which case it's your job to close it after you've gone through.

Keep well clear of the bridge until it's fully open and don't go through until the crew member who has opened it signals that it is OK to do so. With a lift bridge, the person opening it needs to ensure that it is held down while the boat is passing. If it starts to slip, it could come crashing down on the roof of the boat.

Swing bridges and lift bridges can be hard to open (although once they start moving, momentum should make it easier to move them the rest of the way). We believe that opening bridges (and opening locks) is a job for the strongest member or members of the crew (in our case, me!). Children should never be allowed to open bridges by themselves and, if helping to open them, should be very carefully supervised.

Road bridges will require you to put barriers across to stop any traffic before you open them. And if the bridge is carrying a busy road (such as the lift bridge at Aldermaston on the Kennet & Avon Canal, which carries the A340) you may not be able to use it during the morning and evening rush hours.

Once you're through the bridge, if another boat is coming towards you or coming up behind you, it's courteous (not to mention sensible) to leave the bridge open for them. However, you should wait a moment or two to ensure that the boat is actually going to go through the bridge and not turning off into a marina or mooring up before the bridge is reached. If it's not going through, then shutting the bridge is your responsibility.

When shutting a bridge, it is essential to ensure that it is fully shut. Giving it a shove and hoping the momentum will take it all the way is not enough. Stay with the bridge until you hear that 'clunk' that tells you it's safely shut.

Whatever type of bridge you're going through, line up to it well in advance and try to keep to the centre of the channel. If you have to wait for another boat to come through, you should stay over to the right and a fair distance back from the bridge to allow yourself room to manoeuvre when it's your turn.

Tunnels

Some tunnels are wide enough for boats going in opposite directions to pass each other. Some aren't. There will usually be a sign at the mouth of the tunnel with information about this, and we've put some guidance about certain tunnels in Part Two.

As you enter the tunnel, turn on your headlight and a couple of interior lights. There may be a sign telling you to turn off your cabin lights but some people find leaving one or two on can make it easier to judge the distance from the wall. You should also sound a long blast on the horn to let anyone already in there know that you're on your way. A crew member should ensure that the stove is turned off in the galley and that no one is smoking. Travel at a moderate speed - more than tick over and less than full speed - and steer by keeping an eye on one side of the tunnel. However, do not focus entirely on the tunnel wall to the exclusion of all else or you may not see the headlights of an oncoming boat or the canoeist you are about to drown!!!

Move the tiller as little as possible while you're in the tunnel. You may feel that the boat's being pulled to one side but this is an illusion (and a common one). There is usually a wooden buffer along the length of one wall. You can rub along this buffer all the way through if you prefer but - if the buffer's on your left - keep a careful watch out for oncoming boats as you'll have to move over to the right to pass them. If a boat does approach you, coming the other way, keep well over to the right and slow down to tick over well before you pass them. Then, if you need to use a little throttle to help you steer as you get close, you'll still be going slowly enough. If you move your headlight so it's shining towards the right hand wall, you'll avoid dazzling the person steering the other boat.

If you follow another boat into the tunnel, make sure you give it at least two minutes' headstart to allow for the fact that it may go through more slowly than you. Also remember that canoes and other small unpowered boats may be using the tunnel - remain alert!

And finally . . .

Don't be nervous. An experienced narrowboater described boating to us as a "contact sport". You *will* scrape the side of the boat against the bank and against the sides of the lock . . . don't worry about it. However, you will not be popular if you scrape or run into other boats - and you could damage them. Be especially careful around smaller fibreglass craft – if you hit them, they could break. The golden rule "when in doubt, STOP!" usually works.

LOCKS
by John

The purpose of a lock is to allow boats to go up or down hill, with each lock acting as a step between two different water levels. The steeper the hill, the closer together and the deeper the locks are likely be. The mechanism is quite simple. Imagine a rubber duck sitting in an empty bath. Fill the bath with water and the duck will become level with the top of the tub. Let the water out, and the duck will sink back to the lower level. In effect, a lock is just a bathtub (big enough for an enormous rubber duck!) with doors at both ends. Working a lock is quite a simple procedure - in fact, it's harder to explain than to do. As with swing bridges and lift bridges, it is sensible for the strongest member (or members) of the crew - in our case, me - to work the locks. There seems to be a tradition of men steering and women doing the hard work, but that doesn't have to be the case - as Annie will tell you!

Locks will be either for you or against you. The latter doesn't mean that they have any personal animosity towards you - just that you will have either to fill or empty them before you can use them. If a lock is for you, the level will be the same as that on your part of the canal and you can go straight in (assuming, of course, that there isn't a queue).

Narrow canal locks usually have a pair of angled (or mitre) gates at the lower end and a single gate at the top. Broad canal locks (which can take two narrowboats side by side, or one wide barge) generally have double gates at both ends.

Unlike a bath, locks don't have a plug hole. The water is let in or out by paddles which are opened or shut using the winding mechanism next to the gate (more on this in the section on *Working the paddles*).

To work the paddles, you will need a windlass and, in some cases, a key. Ask your hire boat company about keys before you leave the marina. There is some information about specific locks that need keys in Part Two.

Approaching a lock
Depending on the time of year and the canal, there may be a queue for the lock. Although mooring isn't allowed immediately before a lock, if there are several boats, it may be hard to tell where mooring ends and the queue

begins. You can either move slowly down the channel and call out to ask the first person you see, or you can pull in to the towpath side, drop off a crew member, and get them to run ahead to find out.

If you get to a lock and there's a queue or someone is coming through the other way, pull over to the towpath side and tie up loosely, making sure you don't leave a great gap between your boat and the one in front of you. There are usually bollards provided which make it easy to tie up temporarily. Just loop your centre rope round the bollard a couple of times and tie the end to the rail at the back end of the boat, after pulling in the slack. The person steering will then be able to unhook the rope when it's your turn for the lock, without the crew having to walk back to the boat to untie it.

Don't turn the engine off while you're waiting. Because you're only loosely tied you may find you drift slightly but this shouldn't be a problem.

If the queue is a long one, the bollards may all be taken in which case one of your crew will need to stand on the towpath and hold the boat using the centre rope. However, great care should be taken - ropes should never be wrapped round your hand or your body as this could cause serious injury. But, at the same time, they need to be held firmly to prevent them slipping and falling into the canal where they could get wrapped round your propeller. If your crew member is uncertain about holding the boat, it is probably better to use a single pin until you can get to the bollards. If the bank is very overgrown, this may not be possible, so it will be up to the person steering to keep the boat into the side and out of the way of boats coming out of the lock.

Most locks are do-it-yourself but lock keepers are frequently to be found where there are flights or staircase locks. If there is a keeper, he will tell you when to move into the lock.

More often, though, there isn't a keeper. The lock gates are kept shut except when a boat is going in or out so, if there's no queue, a crew member will need to walk up to check whether the lock is in your favour (unless you're lucky enough to get to there just as another boat is coming out towards you, in which case, having dropped off your crew, you can drive straight in). If, however, the lock is against you, you will need to fill it before you can go down or empty it before you can go up.

But BEFORE YOU DO ANYTHING, check whether a boat is approaching the lock from the other direction. A lock that is against you will be for it, so its crew members are not going to be best pleased to find that you've already started to fill or empty the lock, rather than wait a couple of minutes for them to get there. Not only will this not save you any time but it will mean a wait of up to twenty minutes for them - and it is also a waste of water. It may sound strange, but canal water is precious and has to be conserved. The pump installed at the bottom of the Caen Hill Flight of locks on the Kennet & Avon Canal in 1996 returns up to 32 million litres of water to the top of the flight each day. And while a single lock will move far less water downhill, the result is still cumulative. Eventually the upper level could be drained to the point where no boats can move!

Once you're tied up, your crew can then go up to the lock and offer to help the crew of the other boat. They may be doing OK and so not need any help - or they may welcome it with open arms. If a single person is working the lock, it's likely to be the latter! Not only is this helpful to the other boaters, but it will speed things up a bit. In addition, while the two crews are standing around after opening the paddles, waiting for the lock to fill or empty, it's a good time to chat and exchange information on good places to eat, good places to moor, convenient supermarkets and any problems they've encountered further along the canal.

Working the lock gates

The gates are opened and closed using the balance beams (see diagram) and can only be opened when the water level is the same both sides. Even then, it can be quite hard to get them moving.

You will have to walk round the lock to get to the second gate. There is usually a board and handrail along the length of the top gate to allow you to cross, but there is often a footbridge.

Working the paddles

A paddle is said to be 'up' when it is open (letting water through) and 'down' when it is closed.

To fill a lock, you have to open the paddles in the top gate (having first checked that those in the lower gates are closed), and this will allow the water to flow downhill from the upper level of the canal into the lock. To empty a lock, check that the top paddles are closed, then open those in the bottom gates, allowing the water to flow out of the lock and into the lower level of the canal. There are two types of paddles - gate paddles, which work a sort of flap or door in the gate, and ground paddles which control the flow of water through holes low down in the lock wall. The mechanism that opens the ground paddles will be found next to the gate. The gate paddle mechanism - unsurprisingly - is on the gate itself.

A windlass

To wind the paddles up or down, you first have to attach the windlass to the paddle mechanism. Many paddle gears are rack and pinion type. It's important to engage the safety catch before you start winding up the paddles in order to stop them falling accidentally. Always wind slowly. When you've finished winding the paddles up, check that the safety catch is in position and then take off your windlass.

Once the lock is full (or empty - whichever you're trying to achieve) make sure you close the paddles again. To do this, reattach your windlass, wind a little further up, taking the strain with the windlass, and you will then be able to remove the safety catch and wind the paddle down the other way. NEVER let paddles drop - always take time to wind them back down. If you let them drop, they could be damaged and, if that happens, the lock will be unusable and no boats will be able to get through until they're fixed. The only time it's permissible to let a paddle drop is if you need to stop the water flow as a matter of extreme urgency - for example, if someone has fallen into the lock.

Going into the lock

Once the lock is in your favour, your crew will open the gates on your side of the lock to let you move in. (Don't forget to untie your rope from the bollard first!) It's important to make sure you are well lined up with the opening before you reach it. If this means reversing a bit once you're in midstream in order to manoeuvre into the right position, that's fine. Take your time - remember there should never be any hurry on a canal. However, you shouldn't slow down too much . . . you need a little bit of speed in order to be able to control your steering. On the other hand, if you go too fast, you'll collide with the lock walls unless you're very, very good at it (like Annie!).

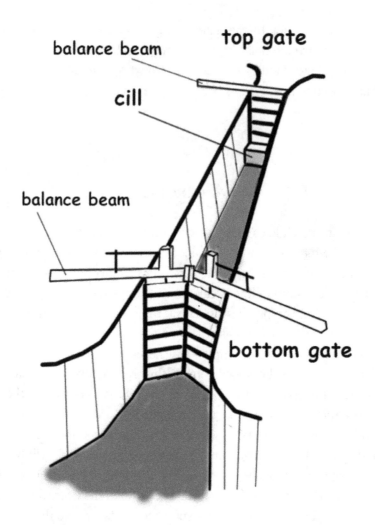

balance beam

top gate

cill

balance beam

bottom gate

Once you're more or less lined up, approach the lock slowly. Some friends tell a story of a couple with whom they shared a flight of broad locks. At each lock, our friends went in first and the other boat came in beside them. At the first lock, the other boat came in much too fast and crashed into the top gates, accompanied by loud expletives from the man driving it. Our friends assumed that the couple were new to narrowboating and hoped for better things at the second lock. But the same thing happened - the boat rushed in, crashed into the gates, and a flow of expletives followed. This continued on up the flight. Eventually they got to the top lock, and as he crashed into the gates for the last time his wife said "I think you're getting better, dear. That crash didn't sound *quite* as loud!"

Crashing into the gates won't do your boat any harm (the gates are wooden) but it can do serious harm to the gates and cause them to become leaky. This not only affects water conservation but can mean that the lock takes longer to fill. If the gate is hit really hard, it may mean that the lock has to be closed while repairs are made. And, while roadworks that close a road can be managed with diversions, you can't divert traffic on a canal.

Once the boat's in the lock, your crew will close the gates behind you. Annie and I disagree about tying the boat up. Annie says:

Do not tie the boat up unless the person at the tiller is nervous about his or her ability to control it. In a narrow lock, other than drifting slightly forward or backward, there's no place for a narrowboat to go. The same is true in a broad lock if you're sharing it with another narrowboat. Even if yours is the only boat in the lock, it's not really a problem if you drift gently over to the other side. If the water is rushing in (or out) and your boat feels it's on a choppy sea it's not because you haven't tied up - it's because your crew has opened the paddles too much and the water is coming in or moving out too fast.

My view (and that of many narrowboaters) is that, if yours is the only boat in a broad lock, it's best to loop the central rope round a bollard. One of your crew then needs to keep hold of it and gently pull it in or let it out as the water level and the boat rise or fall. However, it's important to remember the point I made earlier - ropes should never be wrapped round your hand or your body and they must be held firmly to prevent them slipping and falling into the canal where they could get wrapped round your propeller. And, of course, you should never use knots to tie up a boat in a lock - you must be able to pull it in or pay it out. If you've tied the rope and you haven't left enough slack, your rope or its attachment to the boat may break as the water goes down or, if the rope is very strong, it could impede the steady descent of the boat. Conversely, if you're coming up, the rope will become looser as the water goes up and, with a deep lock, there is a danger that it can get snagged on something and interfere with the boat's movements.

One thing that all boaters (including Annie) agree on is the need to use a rope when you're sharing a lock with a smaller boat. Many small boats are made of fibreglass, which is quite fragile. But, no matter what it's made of, any small boat could easily be crushed in a broad lock by a narrowboat drifting sideways. So, in this instance, keeping the boat on it's own side of the lock is essential. Sometimes it's possible to share a narrow lock, if your boat won't take up the full length of the lock. However, as with sharing in a broad lock, you must go in ahead of the smaller boat and use a rope to ensure you don't drift back and damage it.

Once the boat is comfortably tucked inside the lock, it's over to your crew.

Going down - the steerer

You may think that the steerer's only task is to take the boat into the lock and then take it out the other end. However, when you get your initial training at the marina, you'll be told that, when you are going downhill, you must stay clear of the cill. The cill is a shelf which, if you're going down, will be at the back end of the lock. If you stay too far back, the stern (back end of the boat) can come to rest on the cill and be left high and dry while the bow (front end) keeps going down until it sinks. This idea terrified Annie on our first trip - until she realised that the position of the cill is clearly marked on the side of the lock and there's plenty of room for even the largest boat to get beyond it, although you may have to nuzzle up to the front gates. As the water goes down, keep an eye on the wall and use forward and reverse (very gently and occasionally) to make sure that you stay in roughly the same position and don't drift back too much. This can be quite fun, Annie says! As long as the person manning the lock doesn't let the water out too quickly, you'll probably stay in much the same place anyway and just glide down.

Try to avoid actually touching the gate with the front end of the boat to prevent the chance of your fender catching on it. When the lock has been emptied, wait until your crew has fully opened the gates before moving out. (And, of course, if you have used a rope to steady the boat, don't forget to untie it and stow it carefully before you move.)

Going down - the crew

Once the boat has entered the lock, close the top gate. Open the paddles in the lower gates and allow the water to drain out slowly. You should always open the paddles gradually, whether you're going up or down, and never allow a torrent of water into or out of the lock. A steady flow is quite enough.

Once the water level inside the lock is the same as that in the canal ahead, open the bottom gates so the boat can move out. Close the paddles and, unless there's a boat waiting or coming towards you wanting to use the lock, close the gates. There's a reason for this - lock gates are often leaky, and if you leave one gate open and the other one leaks it could drain the canal above the lock! Closing the gate at least slows this process down.

Going up

Once you've shut the lock gates, you can start to open the paddles. ALWAYS open the ground paddles first and don't let the water go in too quickly as this will cause the boat to surge forward and could flood the front of the boat. Start with a gentle flow and don't open the ground paddles fully until the boat is half way up. Once the boat has risen above the level of the gate paddles, you can open them too. If you open them before this, water could pour down onto the front deck of the boat. Not only would it make a great mess, it could risk sinking the boat! Rarely you may find a lock that only has gate paddles. In such a case, open them very, very slowly and keep the boat as far back from the gate as you can.

Once the lock is full, the water will be at the same level in the lock as in the part of the canal you're moving into, so you'll be able to open the top gates and the boat can be driven out. Before getting back on the boat, the crew should wind down the paddles and close the gates. Remember that you should always wind the paddles down as allowing them to drop back can damage them. Ensure that the gates and paddles are properly closed before you leave. The only exception to this is if a boat is waiting or one is coming towards you, in which case you can leave the gates (but not the paddles!) open, so that it can steer straight in to the lock.

When the gates are fully open (and not before) the driver should start edging the boat forward very gently. Remember, you've got to wait for your crew to finish their tasks before you can pick them up. Keep close to the towpath side once you're out of the lock so they can get on board easily. You should always STEP on and off a boat. If you jump, there's a good chance you'll finish up in the canal! And yes, I confess, on our first trip I jumped. Annie suggested that we put the photo of me being pulled out of the canal on the back cover of this book - but, fortunately, she couldn't find it!

Safety around locks

Locks are probably the most dangerous places on the canals. But if you are careful, there is no reason why you should have any problems.

Perhaps the most obvious danger is the risk of falling in. NEVER leave children or animals unattended near a lock. Be aware that lockside surfaces may be slippery and take care when you are opening gates. Be particularly careful when crossing the lock - if there's a bridge, use it. Otherwise walk carefully along the board attached to the gates and hold the handrail.

If someone should fall in, turn off the engine IMMEDIATELY and throw a lifeline or lifebelt, while the crew closes the paddles. Once this is done, the person in the water may be able to get to the ladder on the lock wall and climb out. If, for some reason, this isn't possible, or if there isn't a ladder, it may be necessary to start to fill the lock again very, VERY slowly, so that the 'swimmer' is gradually brought upwards and can then climb or be pulled out. If the lock is almost empty, it may be better to lower the water - very, very slowly - until it's possible to open the lower gate and pull him or her out using a rope. Finally, if someone falls in, DO NOT jump in to try to rescue them - that just results in the rest of the crew having two people to pull out instead of one.

The second safety factor is one that has already been mentioned - getting the boat stuck on the cill when going down. The cill sticks out by anything up to 5 feet but its edge is always clearly marked in white paint on the side of the lock. Keep your eye on that and make sure the back of the boat is forward of the mark, and you'll have no trouble. However, it is important for the crew to watch the boat as it goes down. If there is any indication that the boat is caught on the cill - either because of its angle or because the person at the tiller is waving frantically - you should immediately close the paddles on the bottom gate and then gently open those on the top gate to let more water into the lock and float the boat off. Once it's free, check for any damage before proceeding any further.

It is also possible, when you're going up, if you're too near one of the gates, to get the front of the boat caught under part of the top gate or the rudder caught between the bottom gates. This won't happen if you keep a distance between the boat and the gates. However, if it should happen, similar rules apply as to getting caught on the cill. Close the paddles immediately and then free the boat (by slowly letting the water out of the lock). Check for any damage before going any further.

We have also talked about the risks involved around ropes and the danger of dropped ropes getting tangled in the propeller, which could disable the boat. Make sure that your ropes are neatly coiled on the deck or the roof, and in no danger of slipping off, before you enter the lock.

A safety factor that is, perhaps, less obvious, but is just as important concerns the windlass. Always keep a firm grip on it and NEVER leave it attached to the paddle gear after you've finished winding up the paddles. It's not unknown for the safety catch to slip and, if that should happen, the paddle gear would slip and the windlass would be spun off into the air and fly into the lock or, far worse, could hit someone and cause serious injury.

Broad locks

If you're on a broad canal, the locks will be able to accommodate two boats side by side. If you are about to use a broad lock and you see another boat approaching, going in the same direction as you, wait for them and share the lock. This saves water and, with two crews working the lock, makes it quicker. Whichever boat is heavier should go in first. If you're both on narrowboats, it doesn't make much difference, but a fibreglass boat could easily be damaged by a large boat entering the lock after it.

If you're the only boat going through a broad lock, your crew only needs to open one gate to let you in and one to let you out, as the space will be quite wide enough for you to get through.

Guillotine gates

These are rare and they tend to be electrically operated. As their name implies, they are lifted vertically to open and lowered to close. The gate has to be lifted and lowered very slowly. If the water seems to be flowing too quickly, close them and start again.

Staircase locks

Usually, if you're going up a staircase, the bottom lock should be empty and the rest full at the start. If you're going down, the top lock should be full and the rest empty. However, Foxton Locks and the Watford Locks (both on the Grand Union Canal) are somewhat different, having been built with side ponds. In these flights you will find two ground paddles at each gate -

one white, one red. The white paddles, which should be opened first, empty the chamber above, while the red paddles fill the chamber below. Quite often there will be a lock keeper at staircase flights, so you can ask advice if necessary.

MOORING
by John

Where to moor

A good up-to-date printed map of your canal should show all the CRT mooring places. Alternatively, if you have a WiFi connection (which, on many places on the canals is poor or non-existent) you can go to the CRT website and have a look at their maps.

Mooring symbol on a map

If you're on a rural canal, you can also moor out in the countryside. However, there are certain places where you must not moor.

The non-towpath side of the canal is usually private property - so don't moor there. You should also avoid mooring anywhere where you might obstruct other boats. So don't moor too close to locks (you are specifically forbidden to use the bollards next to the lock for mooring, other than when you crew is getting the lock ready for you to go in or when there's a queue). And never moor anywhere within a flight of locks - if you start a flight, you have to finish it, so if you want to stop for the night and time's getting on, moor before you get to the flight.

Don't moor on tight bends, close to bridges, or opposite the entrance to a marina or another waterway. If you moor in a CRT stretch of mooring, make sure that you're not next to the water tap - you can only stop there if you're filling up your water tank. From time to time along the canal, you will come to a place where there is a large notch in the bank, on the side opposite to the tow path. This is a winding hole, provided to allow boats to be turned. So never moor in or close to a winding hole.

Angling matches can begin quite early in the morning (anglers like to make full use of the day!) so, as I've already mentioned, if there are signs marking out a stretch for an angling match to take place the next day, don't moor there - unless you want to risk being roused from your bed by irate fishermen.

If there are mooring rings but it's not a CRT mooring, make sure that it isn't private (even if you're on the towpath side). Usually there'll be a sign saying it's private, or displaying the name of a boat, but we once got caught. The canal we were on was a busy one but we'd moored, towards the end of the afternoon, on a stretch with mooring rings - and no 'private' signs. Annie was just starting to cook supper when a chap came along and told us we were in someone's private mooring place. He said he thought the boat owner was away for the weekend - but he wasn't sure. So, as we didn't want to risk having to move later, we had to set off again (about 6.30 in the evening) and it was almost dark before we found somewhere suitable . . . which was quite worrying. We were fairly new to narrowboating at the time (it was only our second trip). If we'd been more experienced we'd have been able to recognise it as a private mooring, even though there were no signs, because there were fenders and tyres hanging over the side of the concreted bank - and that's a sure sign that it's a private mooring.

Very rarely, CRT will have designated mooring for the disabled, indicated by a small badge on the bollard. Like disabled parking, you should not use these places unless you are entitled to do so.

Some stretches of CRT mooring, especially those close to villages or towns, will restrict the length of time you can stay there (most often 24 or 48 hours). If there's no limitation shown, it usually means that you're allowed to stay for up to two weeks.

Finally, be aware that in some places - particularly large towns - the canal will go through some fairly run-down areas. Use common sense when deciding where to moor. If everything looks a bit derelict, don't stop. You don't want to wake up in the morning and find that the boat's been spray-painted with graffiti!

How to moor
Mooring the boat can be quite tricky but, as with everything else on the canal, just take your time and it'll be fine. Having identified where you want to pull in, slow down and, just before the spot, start to turn the front of the boat at a shallow angle towards the bank. Move slowly - but not too slowly.

As with going into locks, you need a little bit of speed to help you steer. After the first few times, you'll get the hang of what the right speed is.

When you're close to the bank, go into reverse to stop the boat, then put the engine in neutral and let your crew off. As always, it's important for the crew to step ashore, not jump - you've got your hands full mooring the boat, you don't want to have to start pulling them out of the canal as well.

If you have more than one crew member and the boat has doors leading to the deck at the front of the boat, one person should step off the front and one off the back, each taking a rope. If there are no doors, they should both step off the back, one with the back rope and the other with the centre rope. They can then pull gently on the ropes to bring the boat in closer to the bank. If you only have one crew member, he or she should step off the front of the boat, since that will be closer to the bank. You can then either do a bit of manoeuvring to bring the back in, or throw a rope to the crew to pull you in.

If you're manoeuvring, it's useful to remember that, to bring the back end in, you need to move forward, but to bring the front end in (as you sometimes need to do if you've swung round too much or if there's a strong wind) you need to put the boat into reverse.

In a popular mooring place, once you're close to the bank, and parallel with it, you may need to move either back or forward before tying up, in order to leave space for other people.

Tying up

Narrowboats have mooring ropes at the front and back, and an additional one in the middle (which is the one you should use if you tie up for just a few minutes with the engine still running - for example if you're waiting to go into a lock).

If the place where you're mooring has bollards or rings, you should tie up to those that are a short distance beyond the front and the back of the boat. Put down the fenders on the towpath side of the boat to prevent scraping (don't forget to take them up again when you set off in the morning or you could lose them) and then tie up securely but not too tightly. Getting the tension right is important - if the ropes are too loose, the boat will bob around every time another vessel goes past.

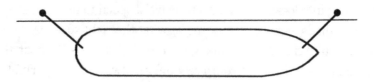

Tied up with front & back ropes

Two mooring ropes (one front, one back) are usually enough for a short stop (lunch or a cup of tea), but for longer stays - particularly if you're planning on leaving the boat for a while - it's a good idea to add the third (centre) rope to make absolutely certain it's securely tied.

If there aren't any bollards or rings, you will have to use mooring pins to attach your ropes to. However, you need to ascertain that the ground is suitable. Obviously, they can't be used in concrete or similar hard surfaces. But, equally, they shouldn't be used where the ground is very soft or wet, because they could pull out. Check that there aren't any obvious signs of underground pipes or cables, then hammer the pins in to about three quarters of their length as far away from the edge of the canal as possible, bearing in mind that neither the pins nor your mooring ropes should ever encroach on the towpath, as that could result in injury to cyclists or walkers.

Make sure the pins are in firmly before you attach the ropes. Once you've tied up, put an upturned yoghurt pot (which you sensibly remembered to pack in your luggage) on the top of each so they can be seen in the dark. If you didn't have room to squeeze the pots into your bag, you can use white plastic bags (firmly tied so they don't blow away).

We haven't used mooring pins for years as we prefer hooks, which are much easier. Some hire companies provide these although theirs tend to be a bit lightweight. If you become a regular narrowboater, we suggest you buy your own hooks - and get the sturdiest type you can find. Ours are made from wrought iron - nothing's going to bend *them*!

Mooring hooks & a mooring pin

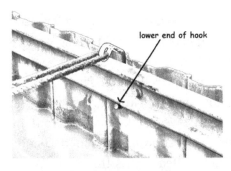

lower end of hook

Hooked on to armco

Away from purpose built moorings, long sections of the canal banks are held in place by an armco barrier. This is much the same as that used for many motorway crash barriers, and for similar reasons - they're strong and they're cheap. And on the waterways they tend not to have to take as much punishment as those on the roads - although that depends on who's steering! On canals, the plates are bolted to uprights with a gap into which the mooring hooks can fit. It's very simple - you pass a mooring rope through the ring on the hook, lower the hook behind the armco plating, make sure it's secure and tie the free end of the rope to your boat, pulling tight.

Tying the ropes
It's almost impossible to demonstrate how to tie ropes using diagrams. So we suggest you have a look at the video here:

http://www.animatedknots.com/lightermans/#Movie

This makes it very clear how to tie a lighterman's hitch, which is the standard way of tying to a bollard. Other knots and hitches are also demonstrated on the website.

If, after that, you're still not sure, ask the person from the hire company who gives you your training to show you the knots you need.

Mooring in bad weather (with a heigh ho, the wind and the rain!)
Wind can make mooring tricky since narrowboats, being flat bottomed, are easily blown sideways by even a moderate breeze. A strong cross-wind blowing you away from your chosen mooring needs some skill and determination to overcome.

If it's very windy (or if strong winds are forecast) try to avoid exposed moorings, especially for overnight stops. You may get in all right but still have trouble in the morning when the wind insists on pushing you back into the bank while you're trying to get out into the channel and on your way. There are usually sheltered places to be found near buildings, in cuttings or near stands of trees. Even a thick, high hedge can shelter you and ensure an easy start in the morning.

If it's been raining heavily, make sure that you don't moor by a soft muddy bank (unless there's armco and you're using hooks). If boats passing you are going too fast (in other words, more than tick over), the waves they create will rock your boat with the result that the pins may work loose. And if just one pin parts company with the bank, you could find yourself drifting across the canal.

On one trip on the Trent & Mersey Canal, we had hired a boat from the Shakespeare Line. Pootling along one day, we were warned by an oncoming boat that an unattended narrowboat had drifted across the canal. When we got there, there was enough room to pass it safely. But we could see that it, too, was a Shakespeare Line boat. We decided to help this fellow-Shakespearean. So we tied up and investigated. The boat was still attached to the very soggy bank by a single pin which looked as though it might work loose at any minute. Normally one should never step onto someone else's boat without asking permission but there was no sign of the people who were hiring it. So I got on board, grabbed the rope and pulled the boat in to the bank. We had some spare pins so I was able to secure it firmly. I thought I'd better let them know what had happened - and, anyway, the names of the two boats were a gift. So I left a note saying:

Dear Juliet, I found you drifting and I rescued you. You owe me a mooring pin and a pint. With love, Romeo.

A few final thoughts on mooring

If you moor out in the countryside where there's plenty of space, don't go and moor right next to the only other boat there - they may be enjoying the peace and quiet.

And, talking of peace and quiet, be aware of people living next to the canal and those in nearby boats - so don't run your engine too early in the morning or play music late at night.

When you pull away from a mooring, do make sure that there are no boats approaching you. Remember that narrowboats can't swerve.

It is unlikely that you'll be mooring on a river - at least until you've got a few more trips under your belt - but, if you do, you should always moor facing upstream (which may mean turning round first) and then fix your upstream rope first. You may need to use an anchor - and you should remember, when tying up, that rivers rise and fall so what might be the right amount of slack in the evening could turn out to be too much or too little the following morning.

SAFETY ON THE CANAL
by Annie

Safety while cruising

- Beware of low bridges. Remember that water levels can rise, particularly after heavy rain. Always keep to the centre of the channel when going under a bridge, and ensure that there's nothing sticking up from your roof that could get caught.
- Beware of cross-winds. You may need to steer at an angle into the wind to stop the boat being blown off course.
- Be aware that there may be strong currents at locks and weirs.
- If you're approaching a blind bridge, bend or junction, give a long blast on your horn to let others know you're there - and listen for answering blasts.
- Never sit or stand or lie on the roof when you're under way. Narrowboats are flat-bottomed and if they become top heavy they can roll over. And never dangle your legs or arms over the side or stick your head out of the side hatch.
- If an impact is likely - with a boat, bridge, lock or whatever - never try to fend it off using your arms or legs or a boat pole. Narrowboats are pretty tough and they have fenders back and front (it's only those at the side you should take up while under way).
- Be careful when using ropes - never wrap them round your hands or your body. A sudden jerk from the boat could cause you serious injury.
- Although you can use ropes to pull the boat in to the side when you're mooring, never try to use them to stop the boat - that's what reverse gear is for!
- If you're walking along the gunwales (pronounced 'gunnels') - the ledges along the side of the boat - hold on to the hand rail all the time. Only use the gunwales if you have to.
- Watch out for smaller boats and debris in the canal. Keep as far away from them as possible and, if you're passing them, do so very slowly.
- And, of course, as with driving a car, don't drink and drive.

Safety in locks

Most of this has been covered in the section on locks, so this is just a summary:

- Make sure at all times that the boat is level and not caught on anything. If in doubt, stop filling (or emptying) the lock and check.
- Keep the boat well away from the cill, and make sure it's not touching the gates.
- Open the paddles slowly.
- At least one person must remain on the boat, at the tiller, all the time the boat is going through the lock.
- NEVER leave children or animals unattended near a lock.
- Be aware that lockside surfaces may be slippery and take care when you are opening gates.
- Be particularly careful when crossing the lock - if there's a bridge, use it. Otherwise walk carefully along the board attached to the gates & hold the handrail.
- If someone should fall in, turn the engine off immediately and throw a lifeline or lifebelt, while the crew close the paddles. DO NOT jump in to try to rescue them.
- Make sure there is no danger of your ropes slipping into the water, where they could foul your propeller.
- Always keep a firm grip on your windlass and never leave it attached to the paddle gear after you've wound up the paddles.
- Watch out for bystanders (otherwise known as gongoozlers) and don't be afraid to ask them to move if they're in your way. If they offer to help, don't allow them to do so unsupervised.

Inside the boat

The cooker, fridge and heaters all use bottled gas. The engine uses diesel. The precautions are exactly the same as you'd take in your home or in your car. If you can smell gas or diesel, quickly check to see if you can see where it's coming from (you may just have left the stove on without lighting it) and, if it's not immediately remediable, close the shut-off valves, open the windows, put out all naked flames (including pilot lights), stop the boat, get off and then 'phone the hire company. Don't switch anything electrical on or off (and that includes the lights and the bilge pump) until you're sure that the last whiff has dispersed.

186

If anyone on board starts to experience headaches, tiredness, sickness, dizziness or other flu-like symptoms, particularly if he or she looks quite flushed, it could be the result of carbon monoxide fumes. To avoid this risk, always ensure that the ventilators remain unobstructed and open windows whenever possible. If you are concerned that someone has been affected, seek medical attention immediately and, if it's proved to be carbon monoxide poisoning, you should contact the hire company before taking the boat any further.

All boats carry fire blankets and fire extinguishers. But in the unlikely case of a serious fire, jump overboard - having first checked that the waterway is clear. Most canals are fairly shallow, and it's easy to forget that it's better to get wet than to get burnt.

Life jackets
These are always supplied but, in fact, they usually only need to be worn by:
- children
- non-swimmers
- anyone who is disabled

Most canals are very shallow and, since most people who fall in do so because they're jumping from the boat to the bank, they'll be in the shallowest section and should be able to stand up. If they fall into the deeper part of the canal, they may need to swim a stroke or two to get to the bank, although even this may not be necessary as the water probably won't be more than about 4 feet deep. However (and this is an important 'however') there are some canals (such as the Caledonian Canal in Scotland) that are deeper and where life jackets may be advisable. Be guided by the person who gives you your initial training.

What to do if someone falls in
- Do not panic and do not jump in after them - that just results in two very wet people rather than one.
- Take the engine out of gear immediately and DO NOT REVERSE the boat as this could drag the 'swimmer' into the propeller.
- Throw them a line or a lifebelt and suggest they try to stand up. The chances are that they'll be able to and can just walk out.
- If you're in a broad canal, it may be easier for them to swim to the side of the boat and be pulled aboard.

- Once back on board, the 'swimmer' should shower and change IMMEDIATELY and any scratches or cuts should be treated with antiseptic.

There is an infection called Weil's disease which - very rarely - can be caught from immersion in canal water. The chances of this happening are minimal but, if you should develop a 'flu-like illness within two weeks of falling in, mention it to your doctor to make sure that - if you've caught it - it's diagnosed and treated promptly.

Other safety factors

Other factors are just common sense.
- Be careful if you're walking along a towpath in the dark. Take a torch (there should be one on the boat) and watch out for mooring ropes and pins, dangling branches from trees and shrubs, and wet patches where you could slip.
- Keep valuables out of sight - if you leave the boat, draw the curtains on the towpath side.
- If you leave the boat in the evening and it's going to be dark before you return, draw all the curtains and leave a couple of lights on.
- If you leave the boat, be sure to lock it - even if it's only for a few minutes. You wouldn't leave your car unlocked and unattended. And if the boat should be stolen or vandalised, you'd be liable for a lot more money than the cost of a car.
- Similarly, make sure you lock the hatches when you go to bed. You wouldn't leave the front door of your house open overnight - and while the canal may seem very quiet, you have no idea of who's around.

WINDING
by John

What does 'winding' mean?

To wind (pronounced as in breeze, gale or hurricane) means to turn a narrowboat around. Most parts of the British canal system are too narrow to allow anything other than short boats to turn, so every few miles a 'winding hole' - or v-shaped inlet - will be provided on the opposite side of the canal to the towpath. The maximum length of boats that can use a particular canal is determined by the size of the locks, and winding holes will usually accommodate the largest of these. However, very occasionally, this is not the case - for example, the winding hole at Tarleton on the Rufford Branch of the Leeds & Liverpool Canal.

There has been a lot of debate as to where the word 'wind' comes from. The most picturesque explanation says that the old horse-drawn boats used the wind to help turn their boats. When you think about it, that doesn't really make sense, as it would be quite easy to turn a boat using just horse power, whereas using just wind power would be impossible if the wind was blowing in the wrong direction.

The most likely derivation (according to the Oxford English Dictionary) is from the Middle English word meaning to turn or to cause to move in a curve. In Shakespeare's *As You Like It*, Touchstone says "Wind away, Begone, I say. I will not to wedding with thee.". The verbs to wander and to wend come from the same root.

How to wind your boat

Turning a boat that's as long as - or longer than - a double decker bus may seem a daunting task to a beginner but, actually, it's quite easy.

Let's suppose that the winding hole you want to use is to the left of you:
1. Approach the winding hole quite slowly – no more than 1 or 2 miles an hour.
2. As you get to the hole, put the tiller hard over to the right AND LEAVE IT THERE. This will turn the boat towards the notch.
3. Then, as the boat approaches the bank, put the motor into reverse to avoid hitting it – STILL KEEPING THE TILLER HARD OVER TO THE

RIGHT. You will notice that the boat keeps turning to the left even when it starts to go backwards.

4. As the rear end nears the towpath bank, put the engine into forward gear to prevent hitting it.

5. And then just keep shunting gently back and forth until the turn is complete.

If the winding hole is on the right, do exactly the same but put the tiller to the left instead of the right. As with everything else on the canal, take your time and all will be well.

It is very satisfying to complete this manoeuvre successfully for the first time and learn how easy a narrowboat is to control if you take things slowly and calmly.

If there's a current (for example, if the hole is below a leaky lock gate) winding may be a bit more tricky. Be aware that some canals, such as the Llangollen, have a steady current at all times. You need to allow for this by starting to turn either earlier or later, as appropriate.

It is probably worth practising turning the boat round at the earliest oportunity on your first trip, to gain experience and confidence.

Other points to consider

If you intend winding and there's another boat close behind you, pull in slightly before the winding hole and signal the boat to go past before you start to turn. That way, you won't be tempted to try to rush because someone's waiting to go through. Similarly, if you're in mid turn and a boat comes along, you may be able to stop momentarily with your front end at the far end of the winding hole, so that they can get past.

But remember, this is not like being in a car. Hold up other drivers on the road and, if you take too long, they'll be hooting you. On a canal, as long as you work slowly and methodically and don't allow yourself to be rushed or panicked, other boat owners will wait patiently - and be impressed at how well you're doing!

If you're approaching a winding hole and are following another boat, stay well back until you see whether it's going straight on or wanting to wind. It will be easier for you to control your boat if you have plenty of room in which to stop and to pull over to the side if you have to wait.

Never . . .

Never moor in or opposite a winding hole. Even on quiet canals, they're in regular use.

Never try to slip past a boat in mid turn unless it has clearly waved you through.

Never turn in the entrance to a marina or moorings unless it is a designated winding point (shown on your map).

Map symbol for a winding hole

MAINTENANCE
by John

Even if you only take a boat for a week, you'll still need to do a bit of maintenance during that time. Don't worry - it's nothing major!

Water

Your boat needs diesel and water. Both tanks will be filled before you set out and - for a trip lasting just a week - you'll have plenty of diesel. However, the water will need topping up. Unless you are a large group or you are very heavy users of water, you'll only need to do this once, about half way through the week, and again at the end of the trip. (Hire companies ask you to top up at the end to reduce their turn-around time.) There are watering points at various places along the canal, some of them near to locks, so you can get a quick fill up while queuing. They will be marked on your map with a tap symbol.

The cap of the water tank is usually on the left of the boat. You'll find it close to the cap of the sewage tank. However, they will both be clearly labelled, so read carefully before opening the tank! The cap is usually on a chain but, if it isn't, be careful how you unscrew it. Make sure you wash the end of your hose before putting it in the tank - you don't want to risk contaminating the water there.

Sometimes there are two taps at a water point but, if they both take water from the same supply, the flow may be slow if they are both turned on at the same time. In this situation, if yours was the second boat to arrive, turn off your tap and let the other boat finish. It could be quicker for both of you.

Make sure that your hose isn't a hazard for cyclists or pedestrians. And as soon as you've finished topping up, move away from the watering point so it's clear for the next boat that wants to use it.

Evening checks

These will be explained when you get your training. They need to be done every night, once you've tied up.
- **Check the weed box.** Take the key out of the ignition to prevent accidents then lift the floor panel at the back of the boat. The weed box is over the

propeller. Lift out the heavy cover and reach down to remove anything that is wrapped round the propeller. Water-weed, string or other debris can often get caught there and will slow the boat down if not removed. If the boat seems sluggish while you're cruising, the weed box may need clearing more often. You may want to take a pair of gardening gloves with you to protect your hands while you're doing this check.

- **Grease the propeller-shaft bearing.** You will find a cylinder with a tap on top of it next to the weed box. Turning the tap two or three times will force grease into the bearing, forming a tight seal. This stops water seeping past the bearing. The grease slowly gets squeezed out while you are cruising.

- **Pump out the bilge.** There is a button on the control panel marked 'Bilge pump'. Press this until all or most of the water which has seeped into the bottom of the boat has been removed.

Pump out

Unless there are a lot of you travelling together, you won't need to do this during a one week trip. For longer trips, or larger crews, you will need to visit a marina or CRT sanitation station that offers this service. It can cost up to £25 but you may find that you will be reimbursed by the hire company.

However, you may not need to pump out if you observe the principle of OPL. This stands for 'other people's loos'. Take every chance you have - visiting a pub or a supermarket or an attraction - of using their customer toilets!

A FEW FINAL THOUGHTS

Most hire boats have a television but you will probably need to retune it each time you move the boat. And, depending on where you are, the reception may be poor and some channels may be inaccessible. Be prepared to have to wait to watch things on iPlayer once you get home. However, if you're happily watching something and the TV suddenly turns itself off, it may be because your battery is low. In this case (as long as you won't be disturbing the neighbours), run your engine for ten minutes or so to top it up.

The water is heated by the engine. If you want to shower in the morning, you'll need to run the engine for ten or fifteen minutes before the water is hot enough. But do think of your neighbours (both in nearby houses as well as on boats) and if you're aiming for an early start, consider showering in the evening rather than running the engine at a time when others may still be sleeping.

Never step onto someone else's boat without their permission.

Don't worry about needing to know technical terms - unlike sailors, narrowboaters are quite happy for you to talk about the 'front' and 'rear' or 'left' and 'right' of the boat.

Before you leave the marina, the hire company will give you a 'phone number on which to contact them in the unlikely event that your boat breaks down. Because reception on some 'phone networks can be poor in places, it's a good idea, if you can, to take two 'phones that use different networks - if you can't get a signal on one, hopefully you'll get a signal on the other.

When you 'phone you will need to describe the problem and say where you are. Since most canal bridges have names or numbers, you will only have to walk to the next bridge to be able to give an exact location. Always 'phone the hire company, even if there's a boat yard nearby - you won't be refunded for any work you have to pay for.

If the problem is a simple one, the breakdown shouldn't delay you too much. Some friends of ours broke down on their second day out. They rang the hire company and sat down, prepared for a long wait. So they were amazed when someone arrived within half an hour. Looking at the map, they realised that, although they had cruised for about nine hours in total, the winding nature of the canal and the speed of a car compared with that of a narrowboat meant that they were still quite close to the marina!

AND IN CONCLUSION . . . we hope you enjoy your narrowboating holiday and will want to do it again. If you've found this book helpful, please consider giving it a review on Amazon.

Annie & John

GLOSSARY

Balance beam - a long, usually wooden, lever which is attached to the top of a lock gate and used to open and close it.

Barge - a wide beamed flat bottomed boat. A narrowboat is NOT a barge and narrowboaters will not thank you for referring to their boats as 'barges'.

Basin - a wide section of water either at the end of or just off a canal.

Chamber - the part of the lock that holds the water.

CRT - Canal & River Trust. A registered charity that oversees and cares for more than 2000 miles of waterways in England and Wales.

CRT key - a key issued by the CRT for opening some locks and bridges as a security measure. Also known as a watermate key or sanitary station key. The same key is used for accessing water points, sanitation stations, rubbish points and other facilities. It is usually found on the same ring as the ignition key, together with keys for opening the caps on the boat's water and sewage tanks.

Flight - a series of locks coming one after the other in quick succession.

Floatation key rings - key rings that enable you to retrieve your keys if you drop them in the canal!

Gates - the doors leading into and out of a lock.

Gongoozler - a bystander; someone who stands and watches. At busy times you may get a number of these and it can be disconcerting. Ignore them! And, if they get in your way when you're working a lock, ask them to move.

Gunwale - pronounced 'gunnel'; the narrow shelf down the side of the boat on which it's possible to walk (carefully and while holding the handrail).

Handcuff key - a T shaped key used to open some locks and bridges as a security measure.

Hooks - an alternative to pins for tying up the boat, these hook round the armco barrier on the canal bank.

Legging - before narrowboats became power-driven, they were towed by horses. But not all tunnels had towpaths and so the boats had to be 'legged' through. The boatmen lay on boards across the width of the boat and literally walked horizontally along the tunnel. It was a very slow and exhausting process.

Paddle - the means by which water is let into or out of a lock. Ground paddles control the flow of water through holes low down in the lock wall while gate paddles work a flap in the gate. They are controlled using mechanisms next to and on the gate.

Pins - metal staves with a loop at one end, used for tying up the boat.

Pound - the level section between locks.

Roving bridge - a bridge that lets a horse towing a boat to cross the canal when the towpath changes sides, without having to be unhitched. This was managed in a variety of ways but frequently by building the bridge of iron, leaving a slot in the middle for the tow rope. This is also known as a split bridge.

Staircase - a series of locks where the boat goes directly from one lock into the next. A staircase is a flight, but a flight is not necessarily a staircase.

Winding - turning the boat. Pronounced with a short 'i', as in 'strong winds'.

Windlass - an instrument used for winding paddle gears and also for opening some gates and bridges.

CPSIA information can be obtained
at www.ICGtesting.com
Printed in the USA
LVHW081358201221
706736LV00010B/123

9 780993 073991